Jimmy and Kristin Scroggins have both the vision and the credibility to speak to the issue of gospel-focused parenting. They have not only reared their children with grace and conviction, but have also taught countless other families how to do so. This book does not rely on any illusions that parenting is simple, or that following a set of abstract instructions will lead to guaranteed results. Instead, this book helps readers to see how the gospel can re-shape the way they love and form their children. This book addresses parenting with conviction, vulnerability, wisdom, humor, and honesty. Parents, and future parents, will be glad they read this book.

Russell Moore, president,
Ethics & Religious Liberty Commission

We like this book a lot, and we do not say that because we dearly love the authors. First, it is full of wisdom and common sense that will greatly benefit any parent. Second, it hits head-on many of the issues twenty-first-century parents are facing. Third, it provides a simple and workable game plan for parenting. Fourth, Jimmy and Kristin know what they are talking about, having raised eight children! We are enthusiastic in our endorsement of this book. Read it and be blessed.

Danny Akin, president, Southeastern Baptist
Theological Seminary and **Charlotte Akin**

Christian parenting is challenging. Multiple, sinful influences debunk most every bedrock conviction held by Bible-believing Christians. Christian parents need help. In their new book, *Full Circle Parenting: A Guide to Crucial Conversations*, Jimmy and Kristin Scroggins provide proven guidelines to help Christian families. Veteran parents themselves, the Scrogginses "get it" when it comes to parenting. Their common-sense, biblically-based, parental encouragement will help guide you through the moral and cultural land mines of today's corrupt culture. We strongly recommend this timely book.

Steve and Donna Gaines, pastor and pastor's wife,
Bellevue Baptist Church

When our sons were teens, Jimmy and Kristin Scroggins were godly, wise voices that spoke into their lives and helped us lead and shape them into the men they are today. That's why we are deeply grateful for their profound wisdom shared in these pages so other parents can learn to lead their children through crucial conversations to comprehend the deep and timeless truths they desperately need to face the intense spiritual, moral, and intellectual challenges of our day. This book is a godsend for Christian families!

Hershael and Tanya York, dean of the School of Theology at
The Southern Baptist Theological Seminary
and Women's Conference Speaker respectively

Full Circle Parenting offers timeless, biblical truths to encourage and equip parents in every season of their God-given journey. With the gospel as the framework and foundation, Jimmy and Kristin candidly share the challenges and joys of guiding children into a thriving relationship with Christ, their families, and future relationships. *Full Circle Parenting* reminds us that Jesus sees, saves, rescues, and restores and that true hope for our families is found in the transforming work of the gospel.

Lynette Ezell, mom of six and
host of *The Adopting & Fostering Home* podcast

FULL CIRCLE
PARENTING

FULL CIRCLE
PARENTING

A GUIDE FOR CRUCIAL
CONVERSATIONS

JIMMY AND **KRISTIN SCROGGINS**
WITH LESLEE BENNETT

B&H
PUBLISHING
NASHVILLE, TENNESSEE

To our children: James and Reilly, Daniel and Mary-Madison, Jeremiah, Isaac, Stephen, Anna Kate, Mary Claire, and Caleb. We are cheering you on as you walk in God's design. We love you dearly.

To our grandchildren: Little James, Willow Kate, and any others to follow (hopefully a lot!). Our love for you knows no bounds. May you always place your hope in God.

Acknowledgments

We have a lot of people to thank because a lot of people have loved us, mentored us, raised us, and helped us along the way in our parenting. Putting parenting ideas into a book is a lot harder than it sounds. And we developed these ideas over many years through observing, reading, and listening to others. Along the way we have read scores of parenting books, hundreds of articles on family life, listened to podcasts, attended seminars and conferences, and heard many, many, many sermons and talks on parenting. We acknowledge that very few, if any, of the parenting concepts in this book are truly original to us. One of our pastors famously wrote about sermon preparation: "I milk a lot of cows, but I make my own butter." Same for us and our parenting material. So it would be fair to say that *Full Circle Parenting* has been a collaborative effort!

Our first and greatest parenting lessons were gained from our own parents, Jim and Jan Scroggins and George and Linda Nail. They brought us into the world, raised us up in the church, taught us to love Jesus, and showed us what godly parenting looked like. Their parenting expertise is validated in the love and lives of their grandchildren.

We all rise up and call them blessed. We also love our siblings so much. Jody, Jonathan, and Kelli are our oldest and greatest friends. We are motivated by their relentless passion for their own children (our nieces and nephews).

Our other parenting mentors are too many to mention. But we feel compelled to acknowledge some very special couples who have had an outsized impact on our lives. Bob and Pam Tebow have known Jimmy since elementary school and Kristin since college. They have given us parenting resources, parenting instruction, and parenting examples. They were especially influential to us when the children were young. Danny and Charlotte Akin and Thom and Nellie Jo Rainer are "boy parents." They showed us and taught us so many critical things about raising boys to be men. We had a front-row seat to the lovable shenanigans of their teenage boys and watched those parents respond with grace, wisdom, and humor to remarkable circumstances. Finally, Kevin and Lynette Ezell have served as life mentors and dear friends for the past twenty-five years. They have "big brothered" and "big sistered" us through our entire parenting journey to this point and continue to help shape our thinking about marriage, parenting, and ministry. Their love, support, and guidance are crucial for Team Scroggins.

We are, of course, thankful for the team at Family Church especially their love, constant encouragement, and Christlike example in all things "family." It is an honor to serve Jesus with these highly gifted, highly committed men and women as we seek to teach the Bible, build families, and love our neighbors in South Florida. They are family to us. They help us build our marriage, disciple our children, and stay true to the gospel of Jesus. In the words of St. Paul, "You are always in our hearts." In particular, our Kids and Families Team at Family Church, as well as the Students and Families Team, has helped to shape and support our discipleship strategy with our children. We are so grateful for the help of our church family. Leslee Bennett, our friend and Family Church colleague, has served as "Lifeway liaison," first-look editor, and all-around project-manager. Without her tireless effort, relentless encouragement, and valuable input we would have never pulled this book together.

We are privileged to work with our editor Taylor Combs and the outstanding publishing team at Lifeway. Taylor's desire to give voice to our parenting ideas combined with his insistence on theological precision has made our writing better and the end product immeasurably improved. Russell Moore also provided significant assistance on some of the more delicate subjects addressed in this book. His parental, pastoral, and theological insights were a huge help to us.

We have also learned so much from parents we have met and interacted with in all four churches we have served—First Baptist Church of Shepherdsville, Kentucky; Grace Baptist Church in Evansville, Indiana; Highview Baptist Church in Louisville, Kentucky; and Family Church in South Florida. We have had the honor of knowing so many incredible parents who demonstrate courage, perseverance, forgiveness, faith, and wisdom every day. Our lives are richer for all of them pouring into us and our children.

Full Circle Parenting

Finally, we are ever grateful to our children. They have been the recipients of our parenting training, the objects of our parenting love, and the victims of our parenting mistakes. Thanks to our married sons, daughters-in-law, and grandchildren: James, Reilly, and Little James; Daniel, Mary-Madison, and Willow Kate. Watching them engage in the adventure of marriage and parenting is one of our very greatest joys. As they care for each other and build their families together, they inspire us to keep on keeping on. And we still have other kids living with us (or away at college): Jeremiah, Isaac, Stephen, Anna Kate, Mary Claire, and Caleb. Over the next decade or so each one of them will leave our household to begin their own. Between now and then we have more conversations to have and more training to give. But we love every day with every one of them—they fill our lives and our house with fun and purpose and potential.

To all of the Scroggins kids and grandkids—we love you and we are on your side no matter what.

Contents

Introduction

Parenting isn't for wimps.
—James Harris Scroggins III

"Parenting isn't for wimps."

That's the advice I (Jimmy) got from my dad when we were in our twenties. We were newly married with our first kid and we really didn't understand what he meant. Parenting seemed like a lot of fun, and it was. It still is. But as we had more children and as our children got older, the challenges got bigger and the stakes got higher. Now I completely understand what my dad was talking about.

We're Jimmy and Kristin Scroggins. We've been married for more than twenty-five years. We have eight children and I pastor a church in South Florida. From the outside looking in, you might think we have an idyllic marriage and perfect children. But we don't. We have a real marriage with its ups and downs. We have real children. Six of them are boys whom we like to call "bucking broncos." Two of them are girls who are sweet but stubborn.

We have to navigate crucial conversations like everyone else. It's not easy and sometimes it breaks our hearts. But we have to do it because it's our job. It's not only our job; it's our joy, because parenting is a God-given privilege.

When one of our sons was about two years old, he toddled into our bedroom and said, "Daddy, I learned how to clean the bathroom, come watch me." To be honest, I had very little interest in watching a two-year-old clean the bathroom. But he wanted me to be proud of him, so I followed him into the bathroom just a few seconds behind.

I walked around the corner and, sure enough, he was actually scrubbing the toilet . . . with my toothbrush. I didn't know whether to laugh, throw up, or be angry. But I said, "Wow, you're doing a great job. How often do you do that?" He smiled proudly and said, "Every day!" Needless to say, I got a new toothbrush and started keeping it in a different place.

> Parenting can be simultaneously fun, challenging, embarrassing, frustrating, joyful, and hilarious. Parenting is extremely rewarding, but it most definitely is not for wimps.

The point is, parenting can be simultaneously fun, challenging, embarrassing, frustrating, joyful, and hilarious. Parenting is extremely rewarding, but it most definitely is not for wimps.

Parenting is challenging because there are no fail-safe parenting formulas. If it were as simple as $A^2 + B^2 = C^2$, then everyone would eventually figure it out. But parenting doesn't work like that. There are no formulas to help us solve parenting problems. Rather than a formula, we need a guide—a guide to help us work through crucial conversations with our kids. This is what the 3 Circles is designed to do.

The 3 Circles is a conversation guide to help parents walk through the inevitable challenges, difficulties, and tense moments of life in a family. Every family looks different. If you're reading this book, you may be married, divorced, or living with someone. You may have biological kids, adopted kids, foster kids, or a blended family. Whatever your family looks like, we believe this conversation guide can help you.

We have had thousands of conversations with parents and with kids about every topic you can imagine. We've had conversations about pornography, alcohol and drugs, the effects of divorce, same-sex attraction, and suicide. We've had kids grow up in our church who have ended up with every initial in the LGBTQ+ spectrum. We have had kids turn to different religions and become atheists. Parents have to navigate all of these situations. You can't go into the fetal position. You can't quit and you can't fall apart. Parenting requires us to manage challenges, disagreements, disobedience, sin, and rebellion.

We also have kids who have grown up to be solid believers serving Jesus as doctors, lawyers, construction workers, musicians, artists, and preachers. They have learned how to walk with God and follow his design for their lives. Christian parents have to have rock-ribbed conviction, nerves of steel, tender hearts, and open arms—all accompanied by a fantastic poker face.

Christian parents have to find a way to have crucial conversations from a biblical perspective and distinctly Christian worldview. But we want to do it in a way where our kids don't feel judged or rejected. We want to keep the relationship with our kids so we can continue to speak into their lives. This is the hardest part for Christian parents. We know we can't force Christianity down our kids' throats. We know they need to make their own decisions about God. The goal of parenting is to raise children that love God, love each other, and love us! If that happens, we're willing to live with varying levels of education, income, social status, etc. The key to it all is knowing how to navigate

> Christian parents have to have rock-ribbed conviction, nerves of steel, tender hearts, and open arms—all accompanied by a fantastic poker face.

these crucial parenting conversations while keeping both the faith and the relationship.

Our goal for this book is to give parents in all life stages a simple tool to help you navigate crucial conversations with your kids. The 3 Circles gives us and others in our church a "conversation map" for challenging situations with kids of all ages. It works with elementary-age children when the stakes are a little lower. It works with teenagers when the stakes are a little higher. It works with adult kids when the stakes seem overwhelmingly high. The 3 Circles gives you a plan to remind yourself and your kids that God has a design for their lives, Jesus died for their sin and brokenness, and God always creates a path toward recovery and restoration.

So what is the 3 Circles? The 3 Circles is a tool we developed in our church in our quest to help people build their families according to God's design. Our church is multigenerational and multicultural. The families in our church all look different. We have rich and poor, educated and uneducated, single moms and dads, divorced moms and dads, blended families, adoptive families, and foster families. We have parents from every racial and ethnic background you can imagine. There are same-sex couples from the community who bring their kids to our church. But in working with all of these families over many years, we've discovered that parents from all these walks of life have many of the same challenges. We've found that the 3 Circles is an effective guide to help parents in diverse situations have effective gospel conversations with their kids. Here's a basic overview of the 3 Circles.

> Our goal for this book is to give parents in all life stages a simple tool to help you navigate crucial conversations with your kids.

3 Circles Conversation Guide

We're all going to encounter problems, issues, and concerns with our kids. It's part of being in a family. You may have a problem that stems from your own personal interaction with them.

They may have a problem with some type of personal sin or temptation. They may have someone sin against them. Whatever it is—the problem has to be addressed. Each one of these problems presents opportunities for responsible parents to have crucial conversations. The 3 Circles serves as a road map for these conversations.

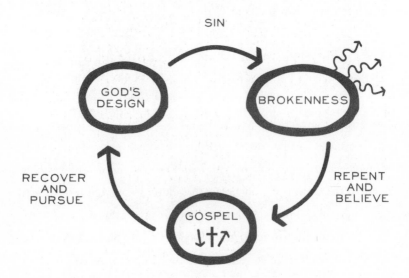

1. **God's Design:** God has a design for every aspect of our lives, including our family life, friend life, sex life, money life, school life, and work life. If we live according to God's design, then we have the opportunity to live in the arena of God's blessing. That is not to say that pursuing God's design exempts us from problems or difficult circumstances.

But it is true that living life according to God's design is a better way to live than the alternatives.

2. **Sin:** God gave mankind a choice: to love God and live according to his design or do life our own way. When we do life our own way, the Bible calls this sin. Our choice is to sin or not to sin—to follow God's design or to pursue alternatives. The Bible points out that every one of us makes sinful choice after sinful choice (Rom. 3:23). We have a built-in tendency to violate God's design. Every problem is a sin problem. It may not be our willful sin or our kid's willful sin. It may be someone sinning against them or problems that arise because we live in a fallen world. But make no mistake—where a problem exists, sin has laid the groundwork.

3. **Brokenness:** When we live our lives in ways that are contrary to God's design, we end up in brokenness. When something is broken, it doesn't work the way it is supposed to work. A sinful life is a broken life. It isn't life the way God designed life to be. Brokenness feels like guilt, shame, anger, and rebellion. Brokenness is just a symptom of the real problem. The real problem is sin. Sin separates us from God and separates us from one another. Sin has experiential, spiritual, and eternal consequences. But God uses the experience of brokenness to get our attention. All of us have experienced brokenness, and the awareness of our brokenness opens us up to the possibility of change.

When we experience brokenness, our first instinct is to try to change ourselves. We look for ways to escape our brokenness, change our situation, and numb our pain. We may try to "white-knuckle it"—reach deep inside of ourselves and exercise willpower to become better people and create a better reality for ourselves. The problem is that when we try to change ourselves, we discover that the changes we make don't go deep enough and don't last long enough. We realize that the kind of change we need has to come from someplace or someone outside of ourselves.

4. **Repent and Believe:** The Bible has a word for the kind of change we really need—the word is *repent.* The word *repent* means to change our minds, change our hearts, and change our direction. We turn away from the sin that created the brokenness we feel, and we turn toward Jesus who can forgive our sins and heal the broken places in our lives. According to the Bible, repentance and belief (faith) go hand in hand (Mark 1:15). We turn *from* sin, we turn *to* Christ, and we believe the story of Jesus. Jesus can bring about change that is deep enough and lasts long enough to truly address our sin and our brokenness.

5. **Gospel:** The gospel is the only solution to our brokenness. The gospel is simply this: the good news that Jesus died on the cross for our sins, he was buried, and God raised him from the dead (1 Cor. 15:3–4). Every person is invited to repent and believe the gospel. If they do, they will be forgiven for all of their sins, Jesus will come into their hearts,

and he will begin to heal the broken places in their lives. The Bible also promises that everyone who believes the gospel will have a home in heaven (John 14:2–3). Applying the truth of the gospel to each situation opens the door to restoration and reconciliation.

6. **Recover and Pursue:** From the moment we believe the gospel, God gives us the power to recover and pursue his design for our lives. God does not change our past. He does not always change painful circumstances. God does not always remove the difficult consequences of our sinful choices. Although our sin has broken our relationship with God, God has made a way for us to be restored to him through the gospel (2 Cor. 5:21). We have the opportunity to recover and pursue God's design from where we are right now. Some parts of our lives may be healed immediately, some may be healed over time, and still others may not be healed until we get to heaven. But whatever the case, we find that pursuing God's design is a better way to live.

The 3 Circles creates a pathway for our conversations. When you encounter a challenge with your child, it helps you build a conversation that addresses the problem, includes the gospel, and gives an opportunity for restoration. The tool isn't meant to be memorized and it isn't meant to box in parents. Because it is a conversation guide, it is adaptable. It is an open-source tool. Parents can include their own experiences or appropriate Bible verses or Bible stories if they think it will help.

The 3 Circles doesn't create flowchart conversations (i.e., "If they say this, then you say that"). It is a guide that many parents have found helpful in working through crucial conversations with their kids. In this book, we will offer stories, personal experiences, biblical principles, and "pro tips" for how to have crucial conversations with your kids. Each chapter of the book will talk you through a different type of challenge that you may face with your children. In each chapter, you will read about real-life conversations that we've had with our own kids or that you may have with yours.

As a parent, you may not encounter every single one of these issues personally, but you are certain to have family, friends, neighbors, and fellow church members who do. Not only that— you will also have to have tough conversations with your kids about topics that aren't covered in this book! That's why a guide is more helpful than a formula. Hopefully, you will be encouraged by these principles and be able to use them to encourage others.

Our lives aren't perfect. Our kids aren't perfect. Our conversations aren't perfect. We have learned a lot up to this point, but we're definitely still learning. This book is our opportunity to share some of what we're learning with you.

CHAPTER 1

God's Design for Parenting

*I don't just want my kids to be moral. I don't just
want them to know all of the biblical rules for behavior. I don't just want them to go through my home
with good grades, no drug addiction, and no premari-
tal sex. I want them to leave my home with a hunger
and passion to know God personally and to be used by
him to accomplish great things for his kingdom.*[1]
—Sally Clarkson

The purpose of biblical parenting is to train our children to know
God, love him, and honor him with their lives. Our goal is heart
transformation, not just behavior modification. We've found that
the vast majority of parenting books—even Christian ones—
tend to focus on behavior modification. Behavior modification is

---

[1] Sally Clarkson, *The Mission of Motherhood: Touching Your Child's
Heart for Eternity* (Colorado Springs: Waterbook Press, 2003), 80.

primarily concerned with controlling kids' actions. We can train our kids to behave and still miss the heart issues. Biblical parenting means going after the heart. We want to teach kids to think about God and pursue his design for their lives. We believe that parents are God's agents to train the hearts of our children. Before we dive into specific crucial conversations or issues we might have while raising our children, we want to consider a few foundational principles to God's design for parenting.

> We can train our kids to behave and still miss the heart issues. Biblical parenting means going after the heart.

God Loves Our Children

"Jesus loves me this I know, for the Bible tells me so . . ." Many of us begin teaching this song to our children before they can even talk. I (Kristin) remember my mom humming and singing this song to me as a young child. Even before I understood the saving power of the gospel and my personal need for salvation, I started to understand the words of this song. It's a simple song full of rich theological truth. God does love our children— even more than we do. He has plans for them and has made them in his image to carry out his purposes. God knows everything about each one of them. He formed them in the womb and put his "thumbprint" on them in a unique way. He continually cares for them and never gets tired of doing so.

The Bible declares God's love for our kids. "Children are a blessing and a gift from the LORD" (Ps. 127:3 CEV). God has a design for his children. It is our distinct privilege and duty, as parents, to help our children understand this design, and to pray they will embrace it. We are their first Bible teachers and give them their first spiritual experiences. Through the Scriptures, we teach them the pattern of God's design, sin, brokenness, and how to be transformed by the gospel. This pattern is important to understand for salvation, but it is equally important as we teach our kids to walk with Christ.

God's love is steadfast and redemptive. The Bible tells us so:

> A person's steps are established by the LORD, and he
> takes pleasure in his way. Though he falls, he will not
> be overwhelmed, because the LORD supports him with
> his hand. (Ps. 37:23–24)

What a comforting and encouraging truth to teach our children. Even though God loves them, parents know that each one of our children needs to be converted. We pray that each one of them will choose to repent of their sins, believe in Jesus for their salvation, and be regenerated by the Holy Spirit.

Even after they become believers, our children will sin. Our children will experience brokenness. Our children will need to learn how to continually repent and remind themselves of the gospel. They will need to know that even though they fall, God will support them with his hand.

This is one of the reasons why the 3 Circles is such a powerful tool. It helps our children understand the gospel to be saved, but it also helps them understand the way the gospel is applied throughout our lives. The 3 Circles illustrates the never-ending opportunity to be restored to their earthly parents, to their other human relationships, and, more importantly, to their heavenly Father.

Parenting Depends on Wisdom, Not Formulas

We already mentioned that parenting is not a formula. For some reason, the futility of formulaic parenting is difficult for our human minds to accept. We want to say, "Here is the problem I'm dealing with as a parent—give me the steps so I can get to the solution."

Maybe we learned to think this way in math class. In 1986, I (Jimmy) was a sophomore at Terry Parker High School in Jacksonville, Florida. My Algebra II teacher was a national teacher of the year. She taught us the Pythagorean Theorem: $A^2 + B^2 = C^2$. That equation is fundamental to mathematics and shows the relationships between the lengths of the sides of a right triangle. The Pythagorean Theorem is foundational to geometry because it works. Every. Single. Time. It works for every person who uses it. No matter your religion, your gender, your ethnicity, or nationality, if you know the length of two sides of a right triangle, it's just "plug and crank." You plug the numbers into the theorem and crank out the answer.

It would be nice if parenting worked like that. But it doesn't.

Unfortunately, too many parenting "experts" and resources put forward the idea that successful parenting is a matter of the right values, perspectives, and techniques. If you just say the right things, use the right methods, and have the right attitude, you can grow every child into a happy, healthy, productive adult. Even Christian parents are sucked into this way of thinking. We all want C^2. We just need someone to tell us A^2 and B^2 so we can plug and crank.

As young parents, we were exposed to various conferences and "systems" for Christian parenting. We received a lot of good teaching in those formats that encouraged us and helped us apply the Scriptures to our little family. They taught us things like how to communicate in our marriage, how to manage our money, how to discipline our children, and how to care for newborns—all good stuff. But the drawback of some of the material was the overconfidence these teachers expressed in their particular combination of theology and methodology. One instructor actually called his scheme a "godly philosophy of parenting." He declared that other perspectives and methods were demonic and required repentance from parents who had been deceived by these dangerous deviations from God's plan for their children. Yikes!

These teachers definitely conveyed an attitude of superiority and condescension toward anyone who disagreed with their guidance. When you believe that parenting is formulaic, then it must mean that those who experience parenting challenges or failures are just too ignorant or too foolish to plug and crank.

Many parents who received the same type of instruction we did later became disillusioned because their kids rebelled as they grew up. They did all the right things, so why didn't their kids turn out the way those teachers promised? Unfortunately, some of these parents didn't understand that the fault was in the formulaic structure of the teaching.

When you have been taught that formulas will work, it is easy for struggling parents to believe that the Bible is unreliable or that God has failed them. Our hope is that readers of this book will reject the formulaic approach to parenting and embrace a more realistic approach based on love, grace, and wisdom.

The Bible is such a great source of parenting instruction because the Bible is realistic about how life really works. Yes, God has a design and, yes, we all fall short of that design. The Bible is full of stories about parents who struggled and fell short. The book of Proverbs offers more direct biblical guidance for parents than any other book. Proverbs was written by Solomon, the wisest man in the world (1 Kings 3:12). We think Proverbs is written as a parenting manual. Solomon is trying to teach his sons how to raise their sons—his grandkids (Prov. 1:8). Solomon primarily offers wisdom he gained by making a lot of mistakes. Even though Solomon was a king who was wealthy and wise, he had many insecurities. He also had lots of unhealthy patterns developed during his dysfunctional childhood. Those patterns affected his parenting.

Solomon's dad, King David, failed as a parent. Solomon was the second-born son of David and Bathsheba (2 Sam. 12:24).

Remember that David murdered Bathsheba's first husband so he could marry her. In addition to the cloud surrounding the relationship between Solomon's parents, Solomon had a constellation of half-brothers and half-sisters from David's many other wives and concubines. Those siblings didn't get along. There was all kinds of rivalry, sexual immorality, violence, and rebellion among Solomon's brothers and sisters (2 Sam. 13–18). The point is that Solomon grew up in a seriously dysfunctional environment, at least by modern standards.

Like his dad, Solomon struggled as a father. He gave in to his sinful, selfish, sexual appetites (1 Kings 11:3). His son, Rehoboam, succeeded him as king and foolishly led Israel into a civil war that split their nation in two. Although God loved Solomon (2 Sam. 12:24) and blessed him in many ways, Solomon replicated the sinful patterns of his dad when it came to building his own household. Solomon was wise, but wisdom is only effective if you apply it. In many cases, Solomon failed to apply wisdom to his parenting.

You might wonder what qualified Solomon to write a parenting manual since he had such a shady background riddled with so many parenting failures. The answer is God. It's the same reason we are qualified to be parents. It's the same reason you are qualified to be a parent. It's because God gave us our children and he has called us to raise them. Even if your background is shaky, and even if you have racked up a list of failures, you are still a key part of God's design for your child's flourishing. If Solomon can write a parenting manual, then we can step up and fill the role to which God has called us. God always gives us the opportunity to recover and pursue his design.

But if there is no formula for how can we parent successfully, what's the secret? The secret is wisdom. Wisdom is the thing that we need for faithful parenting. Solomon wrote Proverbs as an old man. He had learned enough and observed enough and failed enough to realize that wisdom is the most valuable parenting resource. Wisdom is the most precious gift parents can pass on to their children. Proverbs teaches that the most effective concept parents can transmit to future generations is the love and value of wisdom (Prov. 2:2–6; 3:13–18; 4:7).

Some people think wisdom is mystical and mysterious, accessible only to a few enlightened elites. But that's not how the Bible describes it. According to the Bible, wisdom comes from God and is accessible to every person who wishes to discover it. We like to define wisdom as "skill at living life." There are biblical reasons we use this definition. This definition strips away the mysticism that can be attached to the concept and makes it attainable for everyone.

> The Bible is a Holy Spirit-inspired treasure trove of parenting wisdom.

A skill is something that you can acquire, develop, and grow. You can gain skill from observing and listening to the experiences of others, as well as by learning from your own experiences. The Bible is a Holy Spirit-inspired treasure trove of parenting wisdom. Proverbs is chock-full of guidance for parents, and the key parenting concept is wisdom.

The longer you live, the more wisdom you gain. The more wisdom you gain, the more wisdom you can apply. The more wisdom you apply, the more successful your parenting is likely to be. This kind of skill at living life allows you to adapt your words, actions, and methods to each parenting situation.

No two parents are alike, no two children are alike, no two families are alike, and no two parenting conversations are alike. You don't need to search for a formula or a parenting silver bullet—those don't exist. Wisdom does exist, and it is a skill that you can cultivate in your life. This kind of skill helps you to be confident even in tough and tense parenting conversations.

We remember being called to the principal's office when one of our older boys was in first grade. We had never been in that situation before. We were nervous and a little embarrassed. We vacillated between being angry with the teacher and defending our son to being angry with our son and wanting to discipline him. But God was giving us an opportunity to build our parenting skills—our wisdom!

As our other sons grew up, we have unfortunately had numerous opportunities to speak to school officials about their behavior. We've gained a certain kind of confidence in these encounters, and we don't really get nervous anymore. We have learned the balance between standing up for our boys and letting them take their medicine. That's because we have developed wisdom—skill at talking to the school about our children.

Some of you have very young children, and you are reading this and thinking, *These people don't have it together. If they were really good parents, why are their kids always in trouble at school?* We understand why you might think that, because we used to secretly make the same comments about parents that we observed in our church and in our community. We made those comments because when our kids were very young, we actually believed that parenting was going to be formulaic. We would have never said that out loud, but in hindsight, we can see that our quiet, slightly judgmental conversations proved what we really thought. We thought if parents weren't getting C^2, it was because they hadn't figured out how to plug and crank $A^2 + B^2$.

God, having a fantastic sense of humor, allowed our children to grow up a little more and allowed us to discover that we don't even have a clue what A^2 or B^2 are half the time. Parenting isn't about perfecting methods and techniques. It isn't about a formula. It is about acquiring and applying wisdom.

We don't want you to get the wrong idea about our kids. By God's grace, all of our kids are believers and, if you met them, they would make a good first impression. They are hard workers. They do well in school. They are good athletes. They love Jesus and his church. But they didn't start out that way. And they may not all stay that way. Every one of them—like each one of us—is a work in progress. We have learned that any success we have had in parenting is not because of formulas—it is because God has taught us wisdom. He has used his Word, the guidance of the Holy Spirit, many parenting mentors, and our church family. He has allowed us to recover and pursue his design over and over again.

Be More Influenced by God and His Word Than by the World

Influence is such a powerful thing. We are heavily influenced by the people with whom we surround ourselves. Plus, we are greatly influenced by the cultural air that we are breathing all the time. We can't help it! We are like a fish who doesn't know what water is because it's all he knows. He swims around in it all day every day. That's how our culture is—we swim around in it every day, and we don't even realize how much of it we are soaking in. We are all like the frog in the kettle of water that's heating up. We are prone to adjust our thinking and our values to fit into the culture in which we live. We have to be careful because we need to be more influenced by God and his Word than by the culture around us. Our kids need to be taught to discover and pursue God's design for their lives.

When I (Jimmy) was in high school, there was this huge party, and all of my friends were going. I discussed the event with my dad and told him I wanted to go. It was going to be pretty wild and, up to that point, I had never been to a party like that. My parents were Christians, and I was a Christian kid. My faith was really important to me, even as a teenager. My dad told me he didn't think I should go to that party. He told me that he would not forbid me to go, but that he didn't think it was wise for me to go. He knew that there were going to be lots of things going on that I didn't need to be involved in. He knew that I would be around influences that would tempt me and try to persuade me to think the wrong way and do the wrong things. He said, "You can go if you want. But if you go, I am going to pray that you will be thinking about this conversation while you are there and recognizing that what I'm saying is true. And I hope you have a terrible time."

I went to the party and, when I got there, I couldn't get my dad's words out of my mind. He was right. There were lots of things happening that I shouldn't have been involved in. I kept thinking, *This is what my dad was talking about.* And I did have a terrible time! My dad was concerned that I would be more influenced by the people and the culture at that kind of party than I was by God or God's Word.

My dad knew the power of the world around me to influence me. And he was right. If I would have listened to the wisdom of my dad, I would have been able to avoid that episode which brought a degree of brokenness into my life.

If we are going to raise kids who discover and pursue God's design, we are going to have to teach our kids to swim upstream against the flow of the culture around us. Our kids are going to have to learn God's design for sexuality, gender, and family structure. Our kids are going to need to learn God's design for money, material things, and generosity. Our kids will want to embrace God's design for how we see people of other races,

> If we are going to raise kids who discover and pursue God's design, we are going to have to teach our kids to swim upstream against the flow of the culture around us.

ethnicities, and nationalities. Our kids are going to need to grab onto God's design for repentance, forgiveness, and restoration. All of these beliefs and the behaviors that follow will, from time to time, place our kids and our families outside the mainstream of our culture. But we counteract the pull of the culture by demonstrating the powerful truth that God's design is a better way to live.

The Bible warns us to be careful not to think like the world around us (Rom. 12:2). It says to be in the world but not of it (John 17:16). We are called to love the people in the world but to be distinct from them. Believers in Jesus are supposed to be different. We are supposed to live according to God's design. And we are supposed to teach this design to our kids.

A belief in God's design means we believe there is a way God wants us to think. There is a way God wants us to live. God's design means believers aren't supposed to be like everybody else. Jesus said believers should be like salt and light in this world (Matt. 5:13–14). He said God's people should be like a city on a hill (v. 14). As Christian parents, we are going to be different and distinct from other parents. We are going to have to train our kids to be different and distinct from other kids—to be more influenced by God and his Word than by the world around them. This won't be easy, but it will be worth it.

Our Hope Is in the Lord

Our kids don't always follow the script we've written for them. The truth is, we don't always follow our own scripts. We hope things will work out a certain way, and they often don't. We want our kids to follow God's design, and sometimes they don't. We make goals and don't always meet them. We teach and instruct our children, and sometimes they don't do what we say. We envision the way something will turn out and sometimes we're disappointed.

Parenting is full of off-script moments. We find ourselves embarrassed, discouraged, worn out, or afraid. We put all of our hope in our children following our script, and when they don't, we feel hopeless. We say, "This isn't working out as we planned." Or even if it does work out, we say, "What if it doesn't last?" We begin to fear and doubt and long for a better plan. In those parenting moments, we acknowledge that we need something more, something bigger, someone to put our hope in who will not fail us.

The Psalms are a collection of ancient Hebrew songs. Songs are powerful. They express emotion, soothe the soul, teach us, and cause us to remember. Psalm 130 is one of fifteen Psalms of Ascent. These psalms are songs of hope. Many scholars believe that they were sung by Jewish worshipers as they ascended the road to Jerusalem during Passover.[2] God's people would sing

---

[2] John F. Walvoord and Roy B. Zuck, *The Bible Knowledge Commentary: Old Testament Edition* (Colorado Springs: David C. Cook, 1985), 882.

these Psalms of Ascent to remind themselves and their families that their hope could not rest in their circumstances nor in themselves. Their hope must be in God and his design.

> I wait for the Lord; I wait and put my hope in his
> word. I wait for the Lord more than watchmen for
> the morning—more than watchmen for the morning.
> Israel, put your hope in the Lord. For there is faith-
> ful love with the Lord, and with him is redemption in
> abundance. (Ps. 130:5–7)

Can you hear the parents singing the words of this psalm to their children? You can picture the moms holding their daughters' hands and singing these rich verses to them as a reminder that God will do what he says he will do. Perhaps the dads had their young sons on their shoulders as they passed on the stories and truths of their God in song. Wait on the Lord. Hope in his Word. Trust in his steadfast and redemptive love.

Notice the imagery in these verses. You have this watchman, this guard, this soldier doing his job. He is keeping watch over the people, their property, and their possessions. He is vigilant and alert. He doesn't know if trouble will come in the night, but if it does, it's his duty to recognize it and deal with it. The community is counting on him to do his job.

As he walks those walls taking responsibility and looking for danger, he no doubt has many concerns and worries. *Would the enemy come? Would this be the night that disaster strikes?* He would wonder to himself, *Can I defend these walls?* And every night, he would watch for the morning to come so he could be relieved of his duties and let his guard down. He watched for the morning not with an "I hope the morning comes" kind of hope. He watched and longed for the morning with expectation, confidence, and assurance. This is how we are to wait on the Lord and put our hope in him.

How many times has the sun risen since you were born? We're going to go out on a limb and say the sun has risen every single day for your whole life (unless you live in the Arctic Circle). There has not been a single time where the sun failed to come up. If you are forty years old, that means you have seen 14,600 sunrises. As long as you get to wake up tomorrow, you will most assuredly see sunrise number 14,601. We don't worry about the sun rising. We know it will happen. It's predictable. It's certain. It's trustworthy. The sun is going to rise.

Those who trust in the Lord hope with more assurance than that. Look again at Psalm 130:6, "I wait for the Lord *more than* watchmen for the morning—*more than* watchmen for the morning" (emphasis added).

This psalm illustrates and teaches us a necessary parenting lesson. It's not a lesson that we just learn once and never forget. Our hope is not in our job, our position, our marriage, our possessions, our children, or our social status. We continue to learn this lesson again and again as we parent our eight children. It's hard not to put our hope in the success of our children. So much of who we are is wrapped up in who they are. When they hurt, we hurt. When they struggle, we struggle. When they succeed, we are proud to cheer them on. We love them fiercely, but we can't put our hope in them. We can't even depend on our boys to take out the trash or pick up their wet towels off the floor half the time, so putting our hope in them doesn't seem very wise.

> It's hard not to put our hope in the success of our children. So much of who we are is wrapped up in who they are.

There was a time when our parenting confidence was sky-high. We thought we could manage, control, and scheme enough to avoid big struggles with our children. When you have eight children, you learn quickly that they are all so different. Those of you who have multiple children know what we mean. You figure out that certain ones are going to be easier to parent than others. Some are more compliant and teachable while others want to figure everything out on their own (which, for the Scroggins kids, means doing it the hard way).

We already mentioned that one of our older boys had a brazen spirit. We were called to the principal's office when he was in the first grade. He toothpasted his whole cabin at church camp in the second grade. As he got older, he was in fistfights, kicked off the football field, pulled off of basketball courts, and suspended from school. There were times we wished we could go back to second grade when the worst thing he could do was put toothpaste in his friend's sleeping bag.

For a couple of years, we watched our son walk further and further from the Lord. It was frightening and heartbreaking. We got on our knees and prayed. We laid prostrate on the floor with tears streaming down our faces and begged the Lord to work in our boy's heart. And in those moments of crying out to God, he strengthened us. We asked, "God, what if he never comes back to you?" God's answer: "Your hope is in me." "God, what if he does come back, but not until he has done something irrevocable, something with permanent damage?" God's answer: "You watch for the Lord your God."

In those unsure and scary times, God was the only constant hope for our souls. Our hope was not that our son would repent—although we greatly desired that. Our hope had to be in God and his redemptive plan. We believed that if our son would repent, God would restore him and turn his brazen spirit into gospel-boldness. We learned to pray with more confidence because these experiences taught us to trust in God more. We knew we could not make our son follow God, but we could show him unconditional love and model what it looks like to hope in the Lord. This is one of the best gifts we can give to our children. We can allow them to see us live out our faith. It is required of us.

Eventually, our son's story took an upward turn. He came back to the Lord. He repented and began again to pursue God's design for his life. He graduated from The United States Military Academy and is now an officer in the Army. He has a beautiful wife and a growing family. He and his wife love Jesus and are looking forward to raising their children to know and love the Lord. To God be the glory, truly!

We are all tempted to put our hope in things or people other than God. Some of you may have lost hope entirely as you have watched your children sin or struggle. We pray the words of Psalm 130 will remind you that God is with you. He has plans for you that are true and sure. God's redemptive plan that he unveiled for the children of Israel is the same plan he offers to you and to your children. Through the gospel, God makes a way out of brokenness and allows us to recover and pursue his design.

Remember the goal is heart transformation, not behavior modification. God has called us to be the ones who train our kids to know and follow him. This is why it's so important for us to remind ourselves that God's design for parenting is:

- Rooted in God's love.
- Revealed through his wisdom.
- Fueled by his Word.
- Sustained as we put our hope in him alone.

Knowing, believing, and living out these principles will prepare us for what comes next—managing our children's complexity and having a lifetime of crucial conversations.

CHAPTER 2

Children Are Complex

*For I do not understand what I am doing, because I do
not practice what I want to do, but I do what I hate. . . .
For the desire to do what is good is with me, but there is
no ability to do it. For I do not do the good that I want
to do, but I practice the evil that I do not want to do.*
—Romans 7:15, 18–19, the apostle Paul

One of our daughters has such a sweet, tender heart, and for
a while that's all we saw in her. She served others, prayed for
others, and read her Bible without being told to do so. It was just
in her heart to do it.

Then we found out that she was lying about almost everything.

She would lie about things that didn't even matter. One time
we even had to take her to apologize to someone, which is super
embarrassing as parents. We thought, *Wait a minute, she's a fake.* It
rocked our world. How can she be over here praying and reading

her Bible and then go over there to tell lies and talk bad about people?

This is when we realized that our daughter isn't fake, she's complex. She does love the Lord. She does pray. She does read her Bible. She does care deeply about spiritual things and about others. Her heart is to be a missionary! But in that season of life, she was struggling. She was experiencing brokenness in that area of her life. Over time, God has delivered her out of that sinful pattern. He exposed the sin and is helping her recover and pursue his design.

It hasn't just happened with our girls; it's happened with our boys too. As boys grow up, one of the big battles they face is what they look at on their devices. Technology is so powerful, and the internet is always available. They have phones, tablets, and computers. If they don't, then their friends do. It's really hard to control every aspect of all of that. So, occasionally, we've found out that our boys have looked at some things that they shouldn't look at on the internet—at the same time they are serving the Lord. They are singing songs about God and to God when they come to church. They are bringing friends to church. Their friends are getting saved. So how can they do both? How can they be looking at trash on the internet and then do all of these amazing things for the Lord? Are they fakes? We say, "No, they are complex." They are experiencing brokenness in that area of their lives.

As parents we're often dealing with situations like these. We wonder which one is the real kid. Is it the good kid doing the good things that we like? Or is it the kid who has done some things that we're not too happy about? We see this complexity when it comes to working through issues surrounding sexuality, dating, technology, and so many more.

We have found this concept of complexity to be extremely helpful in our own parenting and to other parents who ask us for counsel. Just because a kid is rebellious in one moment does not mean he is insincere when he is kind and respectful in another moment. His rebellion doesn't necessarily negate his respectfulness, nor does a respectful attitude cancel out sinful behavior. The child is complex. The process we're talking about—God's design, sin, brokenness, repentance, belief, the gospel, recovery, and pursuit of God's design—is a complex process. What can we do when we encounter this kind of complexity in our children?

> Just because a kid is rebellious in one moment does not mean he is insincere when he is kind and respectful in another moment.

Remind Kids They Are Made on Purpose, for a Purpose

Our kids are made in God's image, and his grace is on them. They are all different, but they are all made by him and for him. They all have challenges, but they are all made by God. He has created them uniquely with different gifts and talents. He has special purposes for each of them. It is part of our job as parents to help them see that God has specific things for them to do. We always look for ways to point out the goodness of God in our kids' lives. God has a design for their lives, and he wants to use them in great ways.

Our kids need to know that their anatomy, their sexuality, and their gender all have a purpose. Dating has a purpose. Their personalities and their physical characteristics have a purpose. Family and church and friendships all have purpose. Technology, art, athletics—all of these things can be used by God in the lives of our children. Let's help steer them in the right direction. It isn't about what feels good or what everybody else is doing. We want to ask ourselves if the activities our kids engage in help them get on the right trajectory to fulfill God's purposes in their lives.

This conversation about God's purposes starts when they are little and keeps going even when they're married (if they will let you). When they are little you want to point out their unique-ness. You want to point out where you see the goodness of God in their lives. Our daughter who lied also has a missionary heart. So we point that out in her. We tell her that God has given her a gift of being able to do hard things and to have compassion for others. We tell her that we can't wait to see how God is going to use that in her life. We have another one that struggles with some learning issues, but he's the hardest worker and has the most tenacious spirit. So we talk about that. We tell him how we see God using his struggles to give him an amazing drive and ability to be determined and push through things. We know that God is going to use that in his life.

We have to show our kids how God actually made them, and that he made them on purpose, for a purpose.

Our Sin Nature Is the Root of Complexity

Human complexity is a theological issue. It relates to what we believe about sin and our human nature.

Parents get frustrated at their kids because they don't have a solid theology of sin. The whole world tells us that our kids are born good and then corrupted by some combination of bad parenting, worldly influences, peer pressure, and the internet. This is not what the Bible teaches. The Bible teaches that our children are born sinners. You don't have to teach your kids to sin.

Even a kid growing up in the best environment as the biological child of two married, Jesus-loving, church-attending parents will start lying as soon as she figures out how to talk. A two-year-old will take a cookie off the counter and lie about it. It didn't happen because someone else dared him to take the cookie or he watched a kid take a cookie on TV. The sinful idea came from inside himself. Every child has sinful ideas that come from his or her own sinful heart.

> The Bible teaches that our children are born sinners. You don't have to teach your kids to sin.

All kids are sinners who need the gospel. Jimmy is a sinner. Kristin is a sinner. We got together and made more sinners. So in our home we have a bunch of sinners who are giving us grandsinners. We all have sin in our lives. If we don't understand this, we're going to be very frustrated.

When your two-year-old is about to stick his finger in the electrical outlet even though you told him not to, he doesn't have a problem with electricity; he has a problem with sin. When your teenager comes home later than you said, she doesn't have a problem with time; she has a problem with sin.

If you understand this concept, it will change the way you parent your kids. Some people associate this kind of theology with anger, as if understanding your children are sinners will make you more angry at them. We have experienced the exact opposite. When you know your own sinful nature and your children's, it helps you understand what's going on! Now, you won't get so mad. You won't get so frustrated. You won't feel like such a failure. You will just say, "My kid is a sinner." And when other people come down too hard on your kids, you'll step in and say, "Hey listen, we're parenting them. We're training them, but they're sinners. They need the gospel. They need grace. They need to be forgiven. They need to be restored just like you do."

We need to treat our kids the way that God treats them: as sinners in need of the gospel to transform their hearts. We see this in Psalm 103:14, where the psalmist praises God for remembering that we are dust. God is gentle and merciful with us, remembering our weakness. We should do the same for our children.

When we repent and believe the story of the gospel—that Jesus died on the cross for our sins, he was buried, and God raised him from the dead—then God restores us and makes us new. He brings order from the chaos that's in our lives. He helps us recover and pursue his design. This is what we want to replicate in our homes. It's not just so our children can be blessings, or so we can have peace and quiet, it's really about putting the gospel on display in our families.

Parents who fail to recognize the reality, depth, and ugliness of sin in the hearts of their children will be very disappointed. Their kids are going to sin over and over again. They will continue to sin for the rest of their lives. When a two-year-old steals a cookie and lies about it, the stakes aren't very high. As kids get older, the consequences get bigger, and the heartache to parents can be devastating. If you understand that kids are sinners, then you have a framework with which to think about and speak to the complexity of your children.

The whole process of discipline, correction, and restoration is designed to bring the sinful will of the child under control. When the child is young, the sinful will has to be controlled externally by the parents. One day the child will be old enough to experience genuine repentance and faith in Jesus. From that point on, the sinful will can be controlled by the Holy Spirit (of course, during the growing-up years parents still have to help). The goal is that the child will become an adult who is willfully submitted to the Holy Spirit, the authority of God's Word, the encouragement of their church family, and the friendship of their parents, siblings, and other believers. But this process takes time, and it includes disappointment and pain along the way. The process involves the recognition of complexity.

Parents Are Complex Too

If parents are honest, we have to admit that our children aren't the only ones in the house who are complex. Genuine self-reflection will remind us of the complexity within our own hearts. If you are married, your marriage is complex. You have good days and bad days—good seasons and bad seasons. Marriage has its ups and downs, and a lot of that is due to our own sinfulness.

We have been Christians for more than forty years. We've read the Bible many times. We've memorized long portions of it. We are lifelong tithers. We have a happy marriage. And yet, we are complex people too! We have sinful thoughts, desires, and motivations. Sometimes our attitudes are selfish. Sometimes our prayerlessness and lack of intentionality with our own walks with God are disappointing. But we do love Jesus. We do love each other. We do love our children. We do serve our church. We are seeking to grow in our relationship with God. We are complex people just like our kids.

So what does the Bible say about complexity? The apostle Paul wrote about his own sense of his complexity in Romans 7:15, 18–19. Here's what he said:

> For I do not understand what I am doing, because
> I do not practice what I want to do, but I do what I
> hate. . . . For the desire to do what is good is with me,
> but there is no ability to do it. For I do not do the
> good that I want to do, but I practice the evil that I
> do not want to do.

Paul was describing his own struggle with sin. There were times when he wanted to do what pleased God. He had a desire to align his actions with God's design, but he failed repeatedly. He kept departing from God's design. Paul had to be one of the greatest Christians in the history of the world. He wrote thirteen books of the Bible. He started numerous churches. He preached to thousands and thousands of people. He influenced the entire Roman Empire. Certainly, if the apostle Paul observed complexity in his own thoughts and actions, we shouldn't be surprised when we observe complexity in the thoughts and actions of our own children, and in ourselves.

Managing Our Kids' Complexity

We encourage parents to think about complexity in terms of issues to be managed rather than battles to be won. Management means you have issues that you have to shape and constantly tend. You have to keep certain areas in bounds. You're going to try to make them the best that they can be. When dealing with complex issues like technology, sexuality, self-image, identity, and peer pressure, you can't think of them as dragons that you're going to slay and never have to fight again. These are issues that you're going to have to manage, not just right this moment, but for a lifetime.

When I (Jimmy) was a youth pastor, I counseled hundreds of young men about struggles with sexual sin. A book came out that was really popular in Christian circles that described sexual temptations as battles that could be won. I read through that book with those young men and tried to implement its principles (some of which were helpful, some not). Over the years I realized that this put young men in an impossible position.

For most men, struggles with lust and sexuality are lifelong management issues. I came to believe that there are only two types of young men—the kind that admitted to ongoing struggles in this area and the kind that lied about it! I asked a man in his eighties how old he was when he stopped struggling with lust. He told me he would let me know when he got that old! We have to manage sexual sin.

The problem with thinking of sin struggles in terms of battles to be won rather than issues to be managed is that you begin to think of strugglers as losers. That's not what Paul taught at all. Romans 7 describes the struggle. Romans 8 reminds us that we are not condemned (v. 1), we are not separated from God's love (vv. 35–36), and we are more than conquerors in Christ (v. 37). Reminding your kids that there is no condemnation for those in Christ frees them from the guilt and shame that comes when we task ourselves with perfection, but constantly come up short.

Help them see that killing sin is a lifelong task, and relieve them of the pressure of being perfect by tomorrow.

Fight Hard to Build Strong Relationships with Your Kids

As you take time to point out God's goodness in their lives, you're spending time with your children. Again, this has to start when they are young. Young parents who go out on walks, play at the park, swim in the pool, and just have fun together are building relational bridges with their kids. We build the bridges now so that when our kids get older and we have to have hard conversations, our kids already know that we love them. They know that we care about them. They know that we're on their side no matter what. We have to intentionally carve out time with our kids so they are ready to hear what we have to say when things aren't as fun and easy.

We've got to build relational bridges strong enough to bear the weight of the truth that we need to get across in the tough conversations. Somebody's going to come home too late. Somebody's going to get drunk. Somebody's going to get in trouble at school. You might even get the opportunity to talk to a police officer or somebody in the community that you didn't really anticipate talking to because of something that happened with your kids. It's okay. Remember your theology. God's goodness is on them. You know that they are sinners and you're going to have to deal with the consequences of their sin. These tough conversations are just one more opportunity to make that relational bridge a little bit stronger.

Build a Network of Adults and Mentors to Speak into Your Kids' Lives

Parents can't do this alone. We need to band together with other adults and mentors who can speak into our kids' lives. There is power in coming together and saying, "We have similar values. We believe the same things about Jesus. We want the same things for our kids. We want them to be healthy and productive members of society. We want them to be great husbands and wives and moms and dads. We want them to succeed as businessmen and businesswomen and police officers and teachers and missionaries. We want them to do these things, but we need help. We've got to have some other people speaking into their lives." You don't want to be on an island all by yourself when challenges arise. You are going to want some other people to pray with you, to care for you, to cry with you, and to give you some really good advice.

This is where your church family comes in. Parenting is a wonderful calling. Yet, it can be wonderfully hard. We need other believers to rally with us, instruct us, encourage us, and rebuke us. Our children need the same thing. We can't tell you how many times God has used other adults in our church to speak into the lives of our children. Fellow pastors, Bible study leaders, and church friends have had countless conversations with our children. Many times, it's the same conversations we have with them. Our daughter has told us, "Mrs. Virginia said that it's really important to spend time in God's Word every day." Our son has said, "Pastor George told us that we should memorize Scripture." Another daughter said, "Pastor Garrett told me I should keep standing for Christ even when things are hard. It's worth it!" We think, *No kidding—we have told you this stuff a million times!* Sometimes they hear it better from someone other than Mom and Dad. But you keep telling them too.

God has also used Christian parents from other families to reinforce our values. Our daughter said, "Mom, did you know Amy isn't allowed to have social media on her phone either?" Then we said, "See—we aren't the only crazy parents! Her mom and dad have the same rules as we do!" Embrace these relationships.

> Make church a priority. If necessary, say "no" to other activities and say "yes" to your church.

Make church a priority. If necessary, say "no" to other activities and say "yes" to your church. Don't miss out on these resources because your schedule is too busy.

When it's all said and done, remember this: the goodness of God is on your kids, but they are sinners. All of this complexity has to be managed. You can do it, and your church family can help.

CHAPTER 3

Gender, Sexuality, and Marriage

God created marriage. No government subcommit-
tee envisioned it. No social organization developed it.
Marriage was conceived and born in the mind of God.[1]
—Max Lucado

We often begin parenting or marriage conferences by having the audience repeat a humbling phrase after us: "I am dysfunctional." The vast majority of the crowd will participate and often the room has a little nervous laugh afterward. We follow up by saying, "If you have a hard time saying those words—it just shows how dysfunctional you really are!"

When it comes to gender, sexuality, and family structure, we need to acknowledge that we all have issues. We have issues in

---

[1] "90 Famous Quotes by Max Lucado," InspiringQuotes.us, accessed December 4, 2020, https://www.inspiringquotes.us/author/2271-max-lucado/page:3.

our past, from our parents, with our extended family, and with our kids. These days nearly every family has some combination of single people, married people, live-in couples, divorced people, and/or gay or transgender people. It's not just you—it's all of us!

All of this dysfunction leaves people scrambling. We grasp for explanations. We need a framework to help us come to terms with the brokenness we feel as a result of all the dysfunction. Since most people have no foundational beliefs upon which to build their thinking, they look to everything from pop psychology, to sociology, to TV talk show hosts, to astrology, to celebrity advice videos. Our world appears to have literally gone crazy when it comes to discussing gender, sexuality, and family structure. We join in the conversation because our own lives are constantly impacted by brokenness in these areas.

One afternoon some parents sat down in my office. I (Jimmy) only knew them as acquaintances at the time, but I was their pastor. They wanted to talk about a topic so personal that they didn't feel comfortable sharing it with my assistant before the visit. I had no idea what I was about to hear.

"Pastor," the dad said, "I don't know how to say this, but we think our daughter is in a mess and we don't know how to help." He went on to explain that their daughter had gone to a prestigious college out of state. By the end of her freshman year she had come out to her parents as a lesbian. They were upset by this revelation but not entirely shocked. Mom said: "She's always been influenced by popular culture and her friends at school." As college life continued, their daughter developed a serious relationship with a girl at school and the two had plans to marry.

For many Christian parents, this would be crisis enough. But these parents were just getting started. They went on to explain that their daughter was now finished with school and had recently announced she intended to transition to being a man. She wanted to be called by a male name and referred to with male pronouns.

This was all very upsetting for these parents. But the story still wasn't over. When their daughter started the transition process, her girlfriend realized that once the transition was complete—if they stayed together—they would be a straight, white, suburban, married couple. The girlfriend didn't like this because (in her own words) she liked being "queer." The relationship was in jeopardy, and the parents were hoping God would use these challenges to move their daughter back toward God's design.

These church members were grappling with questions about how to handle pronouns, what to do about the wedding, how to manage future visits home, and how to pray for the young couple. They were trying to maintain a loving relationship with their daughter. And on top of all that, they were worried that people in our church would judge them if they heard the story. In today's world, pastoral conversations like that are becoming more and more common.

You may feel like that example is extreme. And for some of us, it is. Yet we all have our own set of conversations that are awkward in our own contexts. If you are raising children, you *will* have a lifetime of conversations about gender, sexuality, and family structure. A few of these conversations might be planned (i.e., having "the" talk, deciding on boundaries for dating, picking out swimsuits, contemplating or celebrating engagements or weddings). But most of these conversations will happen on the fly.

Here are examples of conversation starters we have encountered as parents:

- "How come my wiener gets long sometimes?"
- "Why don't Billy's parents live together anymore?"
- "How can Melana's mom be pregnant when she's not married?"
- "What does 'gay' mean?"
- "What's oral sex?" (Insert slang term used in the actual conversation.)
- "When I was at Cheyanne's house, she showed me some YouTube videos that made me feel weird."

Christian parents have to be ready for these kinds of situations and more. Being up to speed on God's design allows parents to be prepared for *any* conversation about gender, sexuality, or family structure. Regardless of the specific context or circumstance, parents can pivot and make a beeline for God's design.

> If you are raising children, you *will* have a lifetime of conversations about gender, sexuality, and family structure.

- God has a design for bodies and biology.
- God has a design for morality, boundaries, and sexual behavior.
- God's design tells you where corrections need to be made when you discover a sinful incident or habit in the area of sexuality.

Someone who is trained to spot counterfeit money doesn't become an expert on every possible deviation from legitimate currency. They only need to be an expert on real money. They know the markings, the paper, the feel, the ink, the look, etc. They focus on what is true and real. Then when the fake bills show up, they can easily spot the departures from the design of genuine currency.[2]

It would be impossible to write a book that answers every possible question parents might encounter on gender, sexuality, and family structure. It's tempting to try to become an expert on every potential deviation from God's design in these areas. The problem is, you won't be able to stay current—culture, social media, societal trends, and the latest letters on the LBGTQ+ spectrum will change faster than you can google. It is more effective for Christian parents to focus on the beauty, truth, and relative simplicity of God's design for gender, sexuality, and marriage. If we become experts on God's design, we will be equipped

---

[2] For training on identifying counterfeit money, the United States government offers an online course: https://www.uscurrency.gov/modules/custom/usc_training_module/training-module/currency.pdf.

to recognize and address departures from God's design in these areas.

The 3 Circles gives us a framework for guiding all of these conversations. It helps us address the real issues, keep the gospel at the center of the conversation, and provide a clear path to restoration when someone messes up.

So let's talk briefly about God's design. The first three chapters of the Bible give us the basic template to talk about gender, sexuality, and family structure. There are plenty of other places where the Bible addresses these topics. There are biblical stories that offer positive and negative examples in these areas. Without going into great detail about Genesis 1–3, we do need to note that these opening pages of the Bible give us a remarkably clear picture of what God's design entails:

> Then God said, "Let us make man in our image, according to our likeness. They will rule the fish of the sea, the birds of the sky, the livestock, the whole earth, and the creatures that crawl on the earth."
>
> So God created man in his own image; he created him in the image of God; he created them male and female.
>
> God blessed them, and God said to them, "Be fruitful, multiply, fill the earth, and subdue it. Rule the fish of the sea, the birds of the sky, and every creature that crawls on the earth." (Gen. 1:26–28)

In these conversations, you may need to bring in important information that is not explicitly contained in the Bible, but God's design gives you a great place to start, and the 3 Circles concept can help you shape discussions to direct every single conversation (even awkward or painful conversations) toward redemption and restoration. Let's see how we can weave God's design for gender, sexuality, and family structure into these inevitable conversations.

God Has a Design for Gender

The Christian story of creation includes the origin of human maleness and femaleness. When Genesis describes the creation of the first human beings, it reveals three important characteristics of gender: differentiation, equality, and interdependence (or complementarity). Christian parents should begin highlighting these simple concepts from the time kids are learning to talk.

Equality

Parents can show kids of all ages that God designed both males and females in his image. That means that boys and girls are equally valuable, and equally important. Being image-bearers is the most fundamental reality for human beings, and men and women share this equally. Although, as we will see, they have differences, both boys and girls have equal access to God, equally valuable purposes from God, and equally significant opportunities to serve God and other people in this world. Thus, while there is much that differentiates us, there is also much that is the same about us—namely, our value and worth.

This biblical articulation of equality is crucial to Christian understanding of how boys and girls, and men and women, should understand themselves and relate to one another.

Differentiation

One of the most vital components of God's design is that males and females are different. This differentiation includes the concepts of gender and biological sex. God has designed human biology so that a person's gender matches their biological sex.[3] That's why, for the purposes of this book (as well as in our own home and in our church) we use the term "gender" to refer to both gender and sex.

Unfortunately, in our world, these two concepts are often divided as if they refer to two completely different issues. Many people today use "biological sex" to refer to the anatomical and biological differences between males and females, while using "gender" to refer to an individual's perception and presentation of their maleness or femaleness. This is why Christians insist that there are only two genders, intimately and inextricably connected to the two sexes God created—male and female.

---

[3] There are a few rare cases where a person's biological sex is difficult to determine. But these cases are rare and are an unfortunate result of mutations, not a failure of the fundamental design. In these cases, Christian parents should work closely with their doctors and their church families to make difficult decisions and to work toward God's design as best as it can be discerned.

In modern conversations some people even suggest multiple "genders" beyond male and female.[4] You may want to dismiss these notions as "crazy talk." And you wouldn't be wrong. But you and your kids are increasingly bombarded with messages through the educational system and popular culture that will undermine God's design in these areas.

> Satan is inviting our kids to doubt the universality and goodness of God's design.

We must not underestimate the power of these ideas. Just like he did with Adam and Eve in the garden, Satan is inviting our kids to doubt the universality and goodness of God's design.

Christian parents must be prepared to train their children that gender and biological sex are tied together, and that God creates each person as either male or female before he or she is even born. According to the Bible, gender isn't a construct of society nor a choice on the part of the individual. If you are anatomically a boy, then God designed you to live as a male. If you are anatomically a female, then God designed you to live as a female.

Some children, and some adults, grow confused over time about their gender and sexuality. Some kids—even Christian kids—develop strong feelings of gender confusion or same-sex

---

[4] https://www.cosmopolitan.com/sex-love/a20888315/genders-identity-list-definitions/

attraction. When this happens, moms and dads shouldn't shame the child, gloss over the child's feelings, or feel embarrassed about what is going on. These feelings are real, and if they are challenging to you as a parent, imagine how difficult they must be for the child. Parents should lovingly, gently, and clearly point their children to God's design. The church family can help. Counseling can help. Prayer will help. And tools like the 3 Circles can help.

Even though alternatives to God's design may appear simpler and easier, they will turn out to be only more confusing and more damaging to the emotional, psychological, physical, and spiritual health of the child and the family. Christian parents have to hold on to God's design. Every child and every family and every situation is unique, so parents will have to contextualize every conversation. The concept of God's design for differentiation between males and females provides the basis upon which more complicated and nuanced discussions can be built.

Interdependence

Equality and differentiation are clearly present in maleness and femaleness whether a person is single or married. But interdependence finds its greatest expression in the marriage relationship. This is clearly seen in Genesis 1 and 2. God designed marriage to be both a relationship and a partnership. Adam and Eve were supposed to love each other. You can hear the strong attraction and appreciation Adam feels for Eve when he says, "This . . . is bone of my bones and flesh of my flesh" (Gen. 2:23). You can understand the raw desire they felt for one another as they were "naked, yet felt no shame" (Gen. 2:25). You can appreciate the bond they shared as the two "become one flesh" (Gen. 2:24). The Adam and Eve story demonstrates God's design for sexual attraction and consummation—men are supposed to be attracted to women and vice versa. God wants marriage to be a healthy, fun, challenging, growing, exclusive, and exciting relationship.

But marriage is more than a relationship—it is also a partnership. Adam and Eve needed each other. They were a team. They were supposed to "have dominion" (Gen. 1:28 ESV) over every creature and every square inch of the planet. They were supposed to fill the earth with their descendants. And they were supposed to serve as God's managers for everything God created on the earth. All of that dominion-taking and all of that child-raising and all of that creation-managing was too much for one man or one woman to do alone. God put them together as partners.

Parents who are married should be teaching and modeling this kind of relationship to their kids. Ideally, kids will experience the warmth of the relationship between Mom and Dad so that they will believe that healthy marriage is a good, desirable, and achievable ideal. Of course, kids will also see that no marriage is perfect. They can learn a lot from watching Mom and Dad make mistakes!

Married parents should also be teaching and modeling a partnership patterned after God's instructions to Adam and Eve. Dads and moms should be working together every day to pay the bills, keep order in the home, raise their children, serve their community, and participate in their church family. Kids who see God's design for marital partnership modeled by their parents will more easily believe that God's design is possible and desirable for them. Research suggests kids are likely to replicate the patterns they experience in their growing-up years.[5] Kids should be taught from an early age that God's design for marriage includes an interdependence between husbands and wives.

But what about single parents? Single parents have unique challenges when it comes to teaching kids about the design and value of healthy marriage, particularly when it comes to interdependence. In many cases single parents are truly going it alone.

Sometimes the parent has a terrible track record with relationships. Sometimes there was a messy breakup. Sometimes there was abuse. The contexts are too varied to address in this format. Single moms and dads should be careful not to project their own difficult or painful experiences onto their children in a way that undercuts the attractive nature of God's design for marriage. Single parents can and should point kids to the goodness of God's design for marriage.

Single parents may have to be intentional and creative to find healthy models for marriage that their children can observe and seek to emulate. The two best places to look for these types of models are the extended family and the church. Even if good

---

[5] "Shared Beliefs between Parents and Teens," Pew Research Center (September 10, 2020), https://www.pewforum.org/2020/09/10/shared-beliefs-between-parents-and-teens/.

models are scarce in your biological or adoptive family, your church family is full of people from all walks of life who are making marriage work in a healthy way. We would encourage single parents to lean into healthy families with healthy marriages in your church. And we would encourage married couples to make space at the table for single individuals in general and single parents and their children in particular. Just as God wired men and women for interdependence, he has wired the church, with all the different callings and life situations it contains, for interdependence and mutual edification.

Whether you are single or married, it may seem that conversations about gender are a minefield in today's world. Moms and dads need to be prepared to articulate God's design for gender, as well as the powerful concepts of differentiation, equality, and interdependence. While there is a lot of confusion in the world about this topic, Christian parents can speak with clarity and confidence because God speaks clearly to this issue in the very first chapter of the Bible.

When we deal with challenges in the area of gender, sexuality, and family structure, we are usually not talking about "one and done" conversations. These conversations are often extended, sometimes for weeks, months, or years. Some issues may be addressed in a few conversations. Some situations will require the help of doctors, counselors, or therapists. Some kids will have lifelong struggles in certain areas of their sexuality. Some kids will have extremely painful challenges that tempt everyone involved to give up on the goodness of God's design. But don't do it. The alternatives are not better.

Marriage: God's Design for Sexuality and Family Structure

One day, as we were writing this book, I (Jimmy) came home from work. It had been a long day, but I'm always glad to see Kristin and the kids. On this particular day my two teenage daughters were in the kitchen. "Dad!" they said. "What are your top five Disney princess movies?" To be honest, I don't give a lot of thought to Disney princess movies and that's not my preferred movie genre. But to play along, I named favorites: *Cinderella*, *Snow White*, *Frozen 2*, *Beauty and the Beast*, and *Aladdin*.

Of course, as a dad (and a man), I'm thinking, *What difference does it make? It's basically the same story repackaged over and over again.* You know the story line: a young girl faces some kind of adversity caused by an adversary. The adversity often involves some combination of a mistake, misplaced trust, or a false accusation. Through courage, true love, loyalty, and self-sacrifice, the girl is ultimately vindicated and elevated. She is united with a virtuous man who is willing to risk it all for her. Against her initial reservations she falls for him and he for her. True love wins. That's why the stories resonate, not only with my daughters, but with millions of girls around the world.

There is a reason these movies sell hundreds of millions of dollars' worth of tickets and score millions of downloads. It's the same reason our daughters have been planning their weddings since they were three years old. God has hardwired this story into the human psyche. Most of us want to experience love that exhibits bravery, helps us overcome adversity, and stands the test of time, all topped off by deep feelings of attraction and romance.

The good news for our kids is that God's design for most people includes the possibility of this story line coming true. God has a design and a plan for sexuality and marriage that addresses our physical, emotional, psychological, and spiritual needs. God's design doesn't deny the powerful reality of our drives, impulses, and desires in this area. These drives and desires are actually an important aspect of God's design to bless us and make our lives more useful and more meaningful.

The problem is that in our pursuit of true love and sexual fulfillment it is easy to take shortcuts, blaze our own path, and be tempted by the culture around us. Plus, this area of our lives can be really confusing! From the beginning God has declared gender, sexuality, and marriage to be a foundational aspect of his design for human flourishing in this world (Gen. 1:26–28, 2:7, 2:18–24). So it's no surprise that, from the beginning, Satan has attacked human beings in this area.

Genesis 3 tells the story that theologians typically call "the fall." In the fall story, Adam and Eve are commanded by God to take care of the garden of Eden. They were to eat whatever they wanted from any of the trees in the garden with a single exception—the Tree of the Knowledge of Good and Evil. God told them that if they ate from *that* tree they would die. God made his design very clear to Adam and Eve. But the devil came along and began to raise questions about the goodness of God's design for the husband and wife and God's rule about the tree:

> Now the serpent was the most cunning of all the wild animals that the LORD God had made. He said to the woman, "Did God really say, 'You can't eat from any tree in the garden'?"
>
> The woman said to the serpent, "We may eat the fruit from the trees in the garden. But about the fruit of the tree in the middle of the garden, God said, 'You must not eat it or touch it, or you will die.'"
>
> "No! You will certainly not die," the serpent said to the woman. "In fact, God knows that when you eat it your eyes will be opened and you will be like God, knowing good and evil." The woman saw that the tree was good for food and delightful to look at, and that it was desirable for obtaining wisdom. So she took some of its fruit and ate it; she also gave some to her husband, who was with her, and he ate it. Then the eyes of both of them were opened, and they knew they were naked; so they sewed fig leaves together and made coverings for themselves. (Gen. 3:1–7)

Look at what Satan said at the very beginning: "Did God actually say . . . ?" Before there was pornography, prostitution, Twitter, Snapchat, or Tinder, Satan was enticing God's people to question God's design for them.

Genesis 3 shows us the dawning of Satan's best weapons: doubt and pride. He attempted to get Adam and Eve to doubt God's words. Eve recognized the trick though. She knew exactly what God had said and repeated God's Word to the serpent: "God *did* say." So with craftiness and astute understanding of the human heart, Satan fired another dart. He attacked Adam's and Eve's pride. He tempted them to go their own way and to do their own thing—to abandon God's design and commands. They fell for it. They ate from the tree. And brokenness entered the scene of human history for the first time.

> Before there was pornography, prostitution, Twitter, Snapchat, or Tinder, Satan was enticing God's people to question God's design for them.

Ever since that first successful encounter in the garden, Satan has not relented. He tempts us and our children to question God's design and to look elsewhere for answers and satisfaction. Only we have another disadvantage that Adam and Eve didn't have. Because of the doctrine of sin, which we talked about earlier, we're all wired to doubt God's good design automatically. It takes much less work for Satan to trick us now!

Nowhere is this clearer than in the arena of sexuality and marriage. Thus, it is crucial that Christian parents are prepared to inject God's design into all kinds of conversations with our kids. So what are the key components of God's design for sexuality and marriage?

God Invented Marriage

Christian parents must believe this concept and teach it to our children. Marriage is not a societal construct. It is not a tool of the patriarchy. It is not one of many options for happy and healthy family relationships. Marriage is absolutely foundational for human society because marriage was invented by God.

> It is vital that Christian parents see marriage as *the key component* in God's design for sexuality and family structure.

Genesis 1–2 give us the template for Christian marriage. Throughout the Bible we see all kinds of instructions and affirmations that further illuminate God's design for marriage. It is true that not all of our children will be married—some will remain single. But according to research, approximately half of U.S. adults are married[6] and 64 percent say they want to marry at some point.[7] It is vital that Christian parents see marriage as *the key component* in God's design for sexuality and family structure.

---

[6] "As U.S. Marriage Rate Hovers at 50%, Education Gap in Marital Status Widens," Pew Research Center (September 14, 2017), https://www.pewresearch.org/fact-tank/2017/09/14/as-u-s-marriage-rate-hovers-at-50-education-gap-in-marital-status-widens/.

[7] Bella DePaulo, "How Many Americans Want to Be Single? Result of Five Studies," *Psychology Today* (September 20, 2017), https://www.psychologytoday.com/us/blog/living-single/201709/how-many-americans-want-be-single-results-5-studies.

One Man, with One Woman, for Life

If you read the papers or watch the news or get your information about family structure from YouTube or TikTok, then you will be told it doesn't matter what you call a marriage, a relationship, or a family. "It doesn't matter," they say, "love is love." You will be told that everybody gets to make their own choices on family structure, and in a sense that's true. Our society offers people a lot of freedom, especially in America. People have a lot of legal and cultural freedom about how to organize their lives. In many ways, this is actually a good thing.

But when we read the Bible, we see that God's design for family structure *does* matter. And God's design for family structure is very specific and very clear. We like to summarize God's design as "one man, with one woman, for life." This is God's design.

Now some of you read this and say, "Hey wait a minute—that's no good for me because I'm sitting here with my second wife or my third husband. I've already departed from God's design in this area. What am I supposed to do now?"

We know family structure is a sensitive topic. The truth is, none of us have perfect families or perfect pasts or perfect marriages or perfect kids. We all have issues. We are all dysfunctional! We aren't throwing stones because we know that we all live in glass houses. We don't understand all of your stories, and we can't know all of your special circumstances, but we believe that the principles in the Bible have the ability to speak into all of our lives and effectively address all of our unique situations. So our task as Christian parents is to listen to the text of Scripture. The Scripture teaches that God's ideal design is "one man, with one woman, for life."

The Purpose of God's Design

Parents must be prepared to articulate God's purposes for marriage as they engage in conversation after conversation with their kids. A mom or a dad who is not already "scripted up" will appear ill-equipped and uninformed in the eyes of their kids when serious issues are raised in the context of everyday conversations. Fortunately for Christian parents, the Bible is very clear and direct in giving us God's purposes for marriage.

In previous generations, marriage was the norm. Marriage was an expected and necessary part of growing up and participating in society. Until recently, Christian parents didn't have to convince their kids of the value and desirability of marriage. The culture made marriage and childbearing seem important. It was almost inevitable for anyone who wished to be seen as a productive member of the community.

In today's culture, marriage is becoming less and less popular even among Christian young people. On average, men are waiting until they are thirty years old to marry and women are waiting until they are twenty-eight, which is much later than in the past.[8] Fifty-three percent of people are currently getting married,

---

[8] A. W. Geiger and Gretchen Livingston, "8 Facts About Love and Marriage," Pew Research Center (February 13, 2019), https://www.pewre search.org/fact-tank/2019/02/13/8-facts-about-love-and-marriage/.

which is down from fifty-eight percent in 1995.[9] And once they get married, couples are choosing to have fewer kids than ever. According to the CDC, the birthrate in 2018 in the United States was down 2 percent, which is the lowest it's been in thirty-two years.[10]

Positive ideas about marriage and childbearing were once largely transmitted through cultural osmosis. But things have changed. Parents today are likely to be faced with questions or statements like:

- "Why should people wait to have sex until they get married?"
- "What's the big deal about pornography? It doesn't hurt anybody."
- "If you aren't happy, you should get divorced—everybody deserves to be happy."
- "You need to live together for a while before you get married—that way you get to know one another before you make a huge commitment."
- "Marriage is just a way for men to try to control women."

---

[9] Nikki Graf, "Key Findings on Marriage and Cohabitation," Pew Research Center (November 6, 2019), https://www.pewresearch.org/fact-tank/2019/11/06/key-findings-on-marriage-and-cohabitation-in-the-u-s/.

[10] Brady E. Hamilton, Joyce A. Martin, Michelle J. K. Osterman, and Lauren M. Rossen, "Births: Provisional Data for 2018," Vital Statistics Rapid Release; no. 7 (Hyattsville, MD: National Center for Health Statistics, 2019), https://www.cdc.gov/nchs/data/vsrr/vsrr-007-508.pdf.

- "Why would you bring kids into this world when it's so messed up?"

Our kids have to be taught from the Bible that God has purposes for marriage. They have to learn that marriage is good and attractive. Our kids have to see that birthing and raising children is part of God's good design for marriage. These ideas will be increasingly seen as quaint, countercultural, anachronistic, and even dangerous by the culture at large. You only need to google "traditional marriage is anachronistic" to see entries on the first page with titles such as, "Why Do Women Still Change Their Name?," "The Antiquated Tradition of the Marriage Proposal," "It's Time to Legalize Polygamy," and "The Myth of Traditional Marriage." Confusion, along with a shift in conviction, is rampant, to say the least.

If our kids are going to understand and embrace God's design for Christian marriage, Christian parents must be prepared to have frequent, clear, and intentional conversations about God's design. So, what are God's purposes for marriage?

1. Marriage reflects the image and character of God. Genesis 1 tells us that men and women were created in the image of God. So our very humanity reflects who God is. Marriage, when done right, points people to the image, love, and glory of God. Additionally, the New Testament tells us that Christian marriage parallels the relationship between Jesus and the church (Eph. 5:22–33). How so? Jesus loves the church unconditionally, sacrifices himself for her good, forgives her no matter how deeply she offends him, and pursues her no matter how far she drifts or runs away. This is exactly how husbands and wives are supposed to love each other, serve each other, forgive each other, and pursue each other. Over many years and many conversations—these are the kinds of truths that parents should teach children about God's design for marriage.

2. Marriage is meant to make life more fun and more pleasurable. Marriage and family should be fun. Ideally marriage provides a safe relationship where you don't have to fear rejection. Marriage gives you a friend for life. This kind of commitment and friendship provides a platform to face life's challenges and share life's joys. Kids need to be taught that God designed marriage to be a good, positive, and pleasurable relationship.

> A man who finds a wife finds a good thing and
> obtains favor from the LORD. (Prov. 18:22)

3. Marriage is for companionship and help. It wasn't good for Adam to be alone. He needed help to do the things that God had created and called him to do. When a man and woman agree to be married, they commit to stay with one another and help one another for the rest of their lives.

4. Marriage is for sexual fulfillment. Sex between husbands and wives isn't an accommodation to the primitive cravings of human animals. Sex is a beautiful and integral part of God's design of the human body and the marriage relationship. From the time a young person experiences puberty, their sexual desires, urges, impulses, and instincts become heightened and awakened. This is their body getting them ready for marriage.

Sexual desire is part of what drives a man and a woman to commit to a lifelong partnership. The exclusive nature of a monogamous, romantic, and sexual union between husband and wife is God's design for satisfying our legitimate sexual needs. In every conversation about sexuality, even from a *very* young age, parents should point their kids to God's design for sexual fulfillment in the context of marriage. Any sexual expression outside of marriage will not provide the kind of satisfaction for which people are looking. Christian parents should teach their children that marriage provides the only safe, loving, exciting, and satisfying context in which true sexual fulfillment is possible.

> In every conversation about sexuality, even from a *very* young age, parents should point their kids to God's design for sexual fulfillment in the context of marriage.

5. Marriage is to produce and raise children. Christian parents should show their children the opportunity and responsibility to bear and raise children if they are able to do so. The goal is to raise them in the context of a loving, Christian home. The Bible makes it clear that children are blessings, not burdens (Ps. 127:3). And the Bible teaches that it's the parents' responsibility to pass their love for God and their faith in God on to future generations (Deut. 6:1–9). Children are near and dear to the heart of Jesus (Luke 18:15–17). Our goal should be to raise children that aspire to be parents themselves one day, should God give them that opportunity.

6. Marriage is for our sanctification. Marriage is a tool that God uses to make husbands and wives more like Jesus. Marriage can definitely be fun and rewarding, but marriage is also challenging and even painful at times. Marriage exposes our blind spots and our selfishness and our sin in a way that can be extremely humbling. Christian parents should communicate that marriage helps make husbands and wives more like Jesus (Eph. 5:22–31; Rom. 8:29). God has designed marriage for our sanctification.

7. Marriage is to be an outpost of the kingdom of God. When a Christian couple gets married, they form a Christian household. God wants every believing household to be an outpost of the kingdom of God wherever they live. The way they love one another, are faithful to one another, forgive one another, serve one another, and bless others tells their friends, neighbors, and coworkers a story about who God is and what his kingdom is like. When a Christian marriage is at its best, it tells a true and attractive story about God's kingdom. When a Christian marriage and family is at its worst, or when a Christian marriage falls apart, it tells a story about God's kingdom that isn't true or attractive. Christian parents should help their kids see that God's design for the family is part of how God tells the world about who he is. Marriage is an opportunity to live as an outpost of the kingdom of God in this world.

Ways to Model God's Design for Marriage

I (Kristin) don't like clutter. I like tidy spaces and cleared counters—everything in its place. My kids know this about me. Some of them share this love for order and others of them don't.

One Sunday morning several years ago I was getting everyone ready for church. I finished preparing breakfast and headed upstairs to get myself ready. On my way up, I happened to peek in on one of our sons. As I entered his room, I noticed that his closet was anything but tidy. Actually, it was a train wreck. There was a mountain of dirty clothes, trash, an apple core (at least he ate fruit), too many toys, and lots of junk. Clean clothes and dirty clothes were living in the same spot. "You have to clean this up! This is unacceptable," I told him. "Your room looks great, but your closet is the worst!"

I felt so validated in my lecture on the need to be tidy and orderly. It is important, after all. I let him know I would be back in a bit to check on him, and I headed to my room. He said, "Yes, ma'am," and began to straighten things up. I did notice on my way out that though his tone was respectful, his body language showed frustration and discouragement. When I got to my room and opened my own closet, I realized why. Talk about a mess! Although there was no trash or apple cores, it was anything but tidy. There were baskets of clothes that needed folding, stacks of things to take to Goodwill, boxes of out-of-season clothes, and several half-finished projects. Wow! I was immediately convicted.

I realized that my son's closet reflected what I was modeling, not what I was saying. I needed to walk my talk.

We learned early on in our parenting journey that the mantra "do as I say and not as I do" doesn't work very well. Our children tend to imitate what we do—whether good or bad. If we eat junk, so do they. If we yell at other drivers on the road, they yell too. If our closets are messy, their closets are as well. Our children notice everything we do. They notice what is important to us. They sense what we value. And they can easily tell when what we teach is different from what we model. Children, especially teenagers, are fabulous hypocrisy detectors. What we say is important but what we model is even more crucial.

As we model God's design in our own marriages, we give our children a foundation for how to think rightly about God's design. We give them a picture of a relationship to aspire to have one day. We open the door to opportunity after opportunity to talk about God's design for marriage. So, if we know that being marriage-centered is God's design for human sexuality, how do we model it for our children?

1. Pay attention to leaving and cleaving. Leaving and cleaving is a huge part of modeling what it looks like to be truly marriage-centered. Genesis commands that we do it (Gen. 2:24). It is part of God's good and perfect design for boys and girls to grow up to leave their parents for a better and higher relationship—that of husband and wife. As our children see us making our spouse a priority, they will begin to understand how they fit into the family.

71

Two of our sons got married in 2019. They both married wonderful girls. We love our daughters-in-law fiercely. They are absolutely an integral part of the Scroggins family. Our sons have new loyalties now. It is no longer their mom and dad, but their wife who is the primary and most important relationship. If they had to choose between a relationship with us or with their wife, they would choose their wife every time. When they are considering plans and goals, they speak to their wife first. That is exactly as it should be. That is leaving and cleaving.

We are called to model this for our children. This principle not only prepares our children for their future mate, but it also prepares us to release our children one day. There are few things worse than clingy parents who interfere with their married children. We want to always be a part of their lives and available to help them and encourage them as they need, but we don't want to inject ourselves without invitation. We want to help them leave and cleave.

2. Speak positively to your spouse and about your spouse. Our children will likely see the world through our lens. Their view of the world around us and of those living in it is shaped by the things we say. This is why you have first-graders proclaiming their political affiliation at the school lunch table. They don't know a thing about political parties, nor the candidates who represent those parties. They do know, however, who their parents line up with, so that's who they line up with too.

Likewise, the things we say to our spouse and about our spouse impact our children greatly. If we communicate to our children the great things we notice about each other, they notice them too. I (Kristin) know that Jimmy is hardworking, loyal, faithful, and discerning. I want my children to see those things in him and it's my job to point those characteristics out to them. I (Jimmy) know that Kristin is hardworking, wise, patient, and loving. We could dwell on each other's weaknesses, but why would we do that? We want to be faithful to communicate the best things about each other so that our children will believe the best as well, and one day do the same with their spouse.

3. Show affection for each other. Showing affection for our spouses on a regular basis is important. Our children are convinced that we love and enjoy each other when they see us taking the time to be affectionate. It communicates love and admiration for our spouse and reinforces the fact that this relationship is the priority. Our children will act like it annoys them to see us kissing each other or embracing each other too long. Who cares? It is better for them to be a little uncomfortable than to wonder if Mom and Dad even like being together. If this does not come easy for you, work on it anyway. It's worth the work because it provides another layer of confidence and security for children.

4. Healthy sex life. How does a healthy sex life model marriage to our children? Our children shouldn't even know about this part of our marriage, right?

Well, obviously this is a private and intimate part of our marriage only shared with each other. However, it really affects every other area of our marriage. Sex is communication. When we have a healthy sex life, we communicate to our spouse that they are important, that we value them, enjoy them, and want to be with them and only them. When this is right, it makes it so much easier to think of and speak well of one another. It helps us to show affection for each other, and it helps us communicate with each other in other areas. When our spouse feels wanted and cared for physically, they tend to be more willing to communicate about other things. When our spouse is confident that our love, affection, and admiration are exclusively for the other, we tend to be more confident in every area of our relationship. Our children see that this is true and they see the importance of it being so.

5. Pay attention to being on the same page. Lastly, we must make sure we are on the same page with our spouse. This is a huge part of modeling God's design for marriage. This, like all the other things we have mentioned, takes time and intentionality. Our children must know that Mom and Dad are together. There is no way for the child to be in the middle, because Mom and Dad are one unit. Of course, we will have differences of opinion, different outlooks, and different priorities from time to time. But we have to talk about those things behind closed doors and away from the children. Both parents need to be on the same page so that the child knows what to expect. Predictability is key.

Crucial Conversations about Gender, Sexuality, and Family Structure

Of course, no single conversation is going to cover all of these ideas. Parents should know that we are supposed to have a lifetime of conversations with our kids. Wise and well-equipped parents will try to become fluent in the biblical concepts of God's design *ahead of time* so that we will be able to contextualize each conversation. If we wait until these conversations arise before we get our thoughts in order, we will be too late.

Learning the 3 Circles framework will give you a way to think through challenging conversations on the fly, while you draw from your mental library of concepts about God's design.

Start Young

Children can begin learning God's design when they are very young. Parents shouldn't wait for "the" talk—kids need a lifetime of modeling and conversations about gender, sexuality, and family structure. When little boys and girls ask questions about their bodies, parents should respond by pointing them to God's design.

> **Three-year-old boy:** "Why do I have a wiener?"
>
> **Mom:** "Because God made you a boy. And boys grow up to be men, and husbands, and daddies."

Parents should speak clearly to boys about their masculinity and to girls about their femininity. Boys should be taught that God made men to be strong and wise and to work hard so they can protect and help provide for their wife and children. Girls should be taught that God made them special—that one day girls grow up to be women, wives, and mommies. God made women to be strong and wise and to work hard so that they can influence their children and help provide for their families. Kids need thousands of short, age-appropriate conversations that help them learn God's design for their sexuality and appreciate God's design for families.[11]

Plan "The Talk"

Christian parents need to develop a plan for having "the talk" with their kids when the time comes. The talk allows parents to go into detail about God's design for gender, sexuality, and family structure. It also addresses the potential for brokenness in these areas. By having the talk, Christian parents establish themselves as the go-to source for information.

There are excellent resources to help guide parents and kids through this awkward discussion. We have always used Passport to Purity materials from Family Life.[12] This material is excellent. But we recommend you use it exactly as it is written and prescribed. Plan a trip. Do the prework. Do all of the activities. Listen to all the sessions. Use the written guides. You will be

---

[11] Megan K. Beckett, Marc N. Elliott, Steven Martino, David E. Kanouse, Rosalie Corona, David J. Klein, and Mark A. Schuster, "Timing of Parent and Child Communication about Sexuality Relative to Children's Sexual Behaviors," *Pediatrics*, 2008, 34–42, https://pediatrics.aappublications.org/content/pediatrics/125/1/34.full.pdf.

[12] Passport to Purity, Family Life.com, https://shop.familylife.com/t-fl-passport2purity.aspx.

glad you did. Another go-to resource is *Learning about Sex* from Concordia Press.[13]

Minimally, "the" talk needs to include clear, detailed conversation about:

- puberty and body changes
- sexual intercourse and how babies are made
- sexual boundaries
- responding to abuse
- same-sex attraction, gender confusion, and homosexuality
- dating and a plan for how to phase it in
- marriage as the goal for dating and the arena God has designed for sexual satisfaction
- masturbation and pornography
- sexual terms and slang—your kids need to know definitions for things they are hearing out in the world
- how much fun, satisfaction, closeness, and good comes from sexual expression within Christian marriage

Some parents may feel their kids aren't ready for *all* of the information about *all* of the above topics. We understand completely. Parents need to gauge their child's ability to absorb this sensitive information. With our children, we have shared more or less detail on certain issues because we knew they weren't ready. Whatever the case, we recommend that you have the talk before they go through

---

[13] *Learning about Sex*, cph.org, https://www.cph.org/c-2910-learning-about-sex.aspx.

puberty—maybe around ten to eleven years old—and definitely before they start middle school. Considering the reality that kids are exposed to sexually explicit content earlier and earlier, it may even be wise to have an initial talk at seven or eight, and follow it up with another talk to fill in more detail a couple years later.

Understand that even the talk is just an introduction to more conversations. There is no way you can explain everything or answer every question in a single session or even a single weekend. Still, we would encourage you to err on the side of earlier, not later, and more information, not less. You want to get the information to your kids before someone else does. This allows you to present God's design proactively instead of reactively.

As you have the talk (or talks) remember that every one of our children is complex. They will be ready to process these important concepts at different times. They will respond to the information differently. They each have their own set of sexual feelings and experiences and perspectives. That's why they need parents to help navigate them toward God's design.

When it comes to conversations about sexuality, we recommend parents remember that these desires, drives, and impulses must be "managed." Sexuality is not a battle to win but a gift to be managed (see chapter 2). We need to help our kids appreciate the gift, grow it, cultivate it, and manage it. There are times to stir it up and there are times to tamp it down. No matter how mature our kids get or how spiritually committed they are, sexual temptation requires a lifetime of management. You do better some days than you do others. You do better in some seasons of life than you do in others. But you never stop the process of repenting and believing the gospel, recovering and pursuing God's design.

As a part of these conversations, parents need to give their kids room to fail. Sexual temptation is so pervasive that many (if not all) of our children will make sinful choices in this area. Kids will be exposed to pornography. Kids will experiment sexually. Kids will experience same-sex attraction. Kids will experience pregnancy out of wedlock. Our kids will inevitably experience some level of brokenness when it comes to their sexuality.

Christian parents should be intentional about communicating that no matter what happens, there is always a path to restoration. The gospel always makes it possible to recover and pursue God's design. We can forgive and be forgiven. We can change our minds, hearts, and directions. The 3 Circles provides a framework for ongoing conversations between parents and kids about gender, sexuality, and family structure.

Conversations about People Who Aren't Committed to God's Design

Teaching our kids God's design for gender, sexuality, and family structure will create other, more uncomfortable conversations about people in our lives who don't share our perspective. What about neighbors or family members who are cohabitating, are in same-sex relationships, or are having children outside of marriage? The 3 Circles model can help Christian parents have a framework for these types of situations.

Ten-year-old boy: "Why does Aunt Sally sleep in the bed with that lady?"

Dad: "What is God's design for marriage?"

Son: "God made men and women to be married to each other."

Dad: "Yes, that is God's design. Aunt Sally and her friend are kind of living like they are married to each other. It would be better if Aunt Sally was actually married and married to a man because that is God's design. But we love Aunt Sally, and she loves us. Aunt Sally knows what we believe about God's design. We would never want to hurt her feelings, so we don't bring that specific topic up to her unless she asks us about it. We want to be kind and patient with Aunt Sally and her friend. Maybe God will open up an opportunity to talk to them about the gospel! We should pray for Aunt Sally and ask God to help her and encourage her and make her think about his design for her life!"

You can insert virtually any issue into the above conversation. More or less could be said, but you can see the key elements of these conversations: God's design, acknowledgment of sin and brokenness, hope for redemption, our personal love for the people involved, and an encouragement for our kids not to be judgmental or confrontational.

A Sample Conversation Guide for Challenging Questions

As our kids get older, their questions get more challenging. Questions about gender, sexuality, and marriage give parents the opportunity to speak into the lives of our children. We must be careful how we respond. Our child is taking a risk every time they bring hard-to-handle topics to us, and we want to encourage them to keep doing so.

Thirteen-year-old daughter: "When I was at Cheyanne's house, she showed me some YouTube videos that made me feel really weird."

Mom: "Wow, it took courage for you to talk to me about this. I'm so proud of you for telling me and not trying to hide this. What did you see?"

Daughter: "It was several people with their clothes off, doing things with each other."

Mom: "I can see why that would be concerning. I share your concern. Why do you think that bothered you when you saw it?"

Daughter: "I just knew it was wrong to watch something like that. You told me that all of that stuff is supposed to be between a husband and wife, and that it was supposed to be private."

Mom: "I'm so sorry that you saw that and that you have those pictures in your mind. What did you do once the first video popped up?"

Daughter: "I think that is what is making me feel the worst. I didn't turn away. I kept watching. I knew it was wrong, but I just kept staring at the screen. I had never seen anything like that before. I don't know what to do now though. I keep seeing those images in my mind and I feel guilty."

Mom: "One of my favorite things about God's design is that we can always get back on track. I'm grateful for that in my own life. When we sin, we have to remind ourselves of the gospel. We know Jesus died to forgive all our sins. We go to him and ask for forgiveness. God forgives us and helps us move forward. You looked at pornography and that's wrong. I know you didn't seek it out, but now you have seen things that will be hard to forget. I'm so sorry about that. You can let those images remind you there is a better way. When those pictures pop into your mind, turn your thoughts to God and his good plans for you. Pray that he will help you to remember his design and embrace it.

"I do think we need to come up with a plan for what you can do if you are ever in this situation again. It's hard to do the right thing if you haven't planned ahead of time how you will respond."

Daughter: "I think that would help me a lot, Mom. I didn't have a good plan."

Mom: "I love you and I'm always cheering for you. I'm praying that you will know God's design and God's plan for you. He cares for you even more than I do, and he has called you to live for him. If he has called you to do it, then you can do it with his strength."

Notice in this conversation that we introduced the idea of helping our children have a plan in place for managing challenging situations. We will discuss this further in later chapters. We do want to bring it to your attention now, however, because the idea of preparing ahead doesn't just apply to our children. These conversations are tough. They are often awkward and sometimes seem to come out of nowhere. Parents have to prepare our minds ahead of time for these challenging conversations so that we don't have a meltdown when they occur.

> Parents have to prepare our minds ahead of time for these challenging conversations so that we don't have a meltdown when they occur.

Keep the ideas of complexity and management in mind as you navigate challenging situations with your children. Our children are complex, and so are we. Even when they struggle, we want to remind them of the ways God is working in their lives. This will help them press forward. It will help us press forward too.

CHAPTER 4

Technology

> *If you aren't paying for the product—you are the product.*[1]
> —*Social Dilemma*, Netflix, 2020

Technology is a massive challenge for parents. Multiple times a week we have conversations with parents whose kids have gotten into trouble on the internet. It is possible that you picked up this book and turned immediately to this chapter because technology is the burning issue right now in your family. We believe this chapter will encourage you and help you. But because there is a lot of overlap between technology and sexuality, we recommend that these two chapters be read together. So, if you started here, flip back to chapter 3. If you're in the right place, let's dive in.

---

[1] *Social Dilemma*, directed by Jeff Orlowski, written by Jeff Orlowski, Davis Coombe, and Vickie Curtis, featuring Tristan Harris, Jeff Seibert, and Bailey Richardson, released September 9, 2020, on Netflix.

We're old parents—we grew up in the 1970s and 1980s. When we were kids most families had one or two phones, and they were connected to the wall by a cord. Our music came on records, cassette tapes, and CDs. Movies were either at the theater or on a VHS tape. We definitely had access to music with shady lyrics, movies with nudity or sex, and even pornography, but back then it was all physical contraband that had to be acquired, hidden, and then listened to or viewed. You could only watch, look at, and listen to what you could actually get your hands on, so your choices were always limited. Temptation was just as real then as it is today, but parents had a fighting chance to be vigilant and control access. That scenario seems pretty quaint now.

As we are writing this, our world is in the middle of the coronavirus pandemic. Technology-related temptation is kind of like a virus. You can't really defeat it or eradicate it, because a virus will always mutate. Fighting a virus is like playing whack-a-mole—you hammer it down in one place and it pops up in another. That's how tech-temptation is for parents. It's not a battle you can win or an enemy you can kill. It's a sin/temptation arena that must be constantly managed. Our kids will not be able to function in this world without technology, so it's imperative that we, as parents, train them to manage it.

> Our kids will not be able to function in this world without technology, so it's imperative that we, as parents, train them to manage it.

Current and future generations have unprecedented access and unlimited technological choices. The internet makes parental attempts to control choices futile. The cultural, social, and academic environments require even young kids to have wide access to smartphones, tablets, and computers. This combination of access and choices creates a dangerous situation for kids and families.

Some of you reading this book grew up in the 2000s, so you have never known a world without the internet and smartphones and social media. Technology has made parenting infinitely more complex. Every parent has important decisions to make to help their children manage technology.

- When do we let them have a phone?
- Do we set limits for screen time?
- What kind of video games are appropriate?
- When can they use social media? Which apps?
- Do we try to monitor their devices? How?
- What about sexting?
- What about "hook-up" apps?
- What about predators?
- What about bullying?

These are just a few of the issues that parents have to think about in the smartphone/tablet/internet era. As parents manage these types of questions, all kinds of crucial conversations will arise. And our kids will make mistakes along the way. You will have to work through tough situations such as:

- Your child or one of their friends might send inappropriate pictures or messages to other kids. Those can get passed around. It's embarrassing.
- You find out your kid has been doing inappropriate internet searches.
- Your child will be inadvertently exposed to inappropriate material because a friend "ambushed them"—surprised them by showing them a site or video without their consent.
- Your kids will stay up way too late going back and forth with other kids on their phones.
- Your child will visit websites or use apps based around some affinity or interest (writing, art, photography, music, sports, fan-fiction, etc.) and end up being exposed to inappropriate content.
- Your child will discover "work-arounds" for your accountability software using social media apps, Google docs, etc.
- Your child will develop dangerous habits or addictions related to the internet and smart devices.

Every one of these situations, and more, will be encountered by Christian parents today. No matter how hard you try, it is nearly impossible to provide 100 percent protection from bad influences and destructive temptations related to technology. Managing technology is going to require lots of conversations— some of them painful. Parents would do well to think through scenarios ahead of time so that conversations with kids can be upward-looking, encouraging, and redemptive.

Technology management for parents is not a parents-versus-kids battle, even though it may feel like it sometimes. We are actually *for* our kids. Our desire to help them successfully manage technology is a desire to give them a valuable gift. We want them to feel the winning combination of biblical wisdom, Holy Spirit power, church family encouragement, and parental guidance. We want them to be free from the bondage of technology-related addictions. We want them to confidently manage the array of technology-related temptations that will confront them for the rest of their lives. We want them to know the endless availability of restoration, recovery, and redemption when we fall to temptation or fail to manage technology successfully. Mostly, we want our kids to look to God's design as the standard and the gospel as the remedy when we mess up.

Our goal is to help you create a framework for talking about—and managing—technology with your kids.

Challenges for Technology Management

We first began to seriously grapple with the challenges of technology when we were doing youth ministry in the late 1990s and early 2000s. People were getting the internet in their homes. Many of the middle-class kids in our youth group had cell phones with rudimentary texting and crude cameras (smartphones were not a thing yet). Our own children were too young to be affected, but we were seeing problems in our church related to internet pornography, chat rooms, and kids sexting each other. Parents were completely baffled when they would discover this "secret world" that their children were developing online. They were concerned, embarrassed, and frustrated. Since there weren't a lot of resources available, parents were turning to the church for help.

An Ever-Expanding "Secret World"

The truth is, kids have always had a "secret world" where parents and other adults are largely excluded. Previous generations built their secret worlds with phone conversations, handwritten notes, locker rooms, high school parties, music, magazines, slang, and other tools. But the internet exponentially expanded the possibilities and the dangers of the secret world of kids.

As a youth pastor, I (Jimmy) found that parents were generally uninformed about the way young people were using the internet. From time to time, a parent would uncover their kid's internet habits and be shocked at what their son or daughter had gotten into. I had more than one parent in my office say to me, "I'm not even sure I know who this kid *is*." When the parents got a glimpse into the "secret world," it could feel as if their kids were complete strangers.

Kids were upset and felt that their privacy had been violated when parents tried to confront what was going on. Kids were creating a new dimension of "secret world" where authority figures (parents, coaches, teachers, pastors, mentors, etc.) were not present and were not welcome. This secret world largely existed online.

Our church was compelled to start developing guidelines and coaching for parents as they were navigating this brand-new minefield. I developed a word equation to help describe what I saw happening in our suburban, middle class, church families.

Affluence + Technology + Autonomy = Secret World

- **Affluence:** Most of the families in our youth group were not wealthy, but they did have phones, cars, and designer clothes. They had high-speed internet in their homes and multiple computers available to them. Poorer kids didn't have the same temptations because they didn't have that kind of access to technology. The more affluent a family or a society becomes, the more access to technology they will have. Affluence and technology are definitely related. You can only use the tools you can afford.
- **Technology:** Technology is always advancing, so the tools constantly change. The internet has gone from dial-up to high speed in a generation. American households have gone from having a single desktop computer per home to having multiple smart devices per family. Entertainment has gone from physical DVDs to streaming, from websites like MySpace to apps like Facebook, Instagram, and TikTok.

- **Autonomy:** As technology has advanced, parents have grown more and more reticent to police their kids' use of it. Many parents and kids view kids' rooms and devices as almost sacred, private spaces that belong solely to the children. In many families, when parents seek to monitor online activities or devices, it almost feels like the FBI is misusing the Patriot Act. This sense of personal autonomy is unfortunate because it leaves kids to navigate the vast dangers of the internet with little oversight, coaching, or accountability.

Since you know how equations work, you can see that when you increase the values on one side of the equation, the other side increases as well. The result is a larger and more dangerous secret world. Parents cannot eliminate the factors in this equation, and parents will never eliminate the secret worlds of their kids (nor should they, since some of this is just part of growing up). But parents have to be aware that the secret world exists, and parents must be prepared to have constructive conversations about its dangers.

The Ubiquity of Technology

Parents have to acknowledge that technology—namely, the internet and smart devices—is everywhere and unavoidable. Fifty-three percent of kids have their own smartphone by the age of eleven; that number is 84 percent for kids thirteen and up.[2] It is easy to see why. Schools require kids to use email and web-based applications to receive assignments, communicate with teachers, and turn in work. If students participate in extracurricular activities, they have to be involved in group chats or WhatsApp-type conversations in order to interact with teammates and coaches. It's how they keep up with practice or meeting schedules. And that doesn't even account for the immense social pressure that kids feel from other kids. ("What?! Your parents won't let you get a cellphone?"), or pressure that parents feel from other parents ("Get your kid a cellphone! You are making your kid look like a nerd."). So the vast majority of parents are not deciding *if* we are going to manage technology with their kids—we are simply deciding *when* and *how*.

The Ubiquity of Social Media

Social media has created one of the greatest tech-management challenges for parents to date. On average, kids eight to twelve years old use nearly five hours of screen time per day for non-school related activities.[3] Teens average more than seven hours of screen time per day not counting academic work.[4] Much of this time is spent on social media. By far the most popular

---

[2] Anya Kamenetz, "It's a Smartphone Life: More Than Half of U.S. Children Have One," National Public Radio (October 31, 2019), https://www.npr.org/2019/10/31/774838891/its-a-smartphone-life-more-than-half-of-u-s-children-now-have-one.

[3] Ibid.

[4] Ibid.

social media app for kids in these age groups is YouTube. The average teenager watches videos for more than two hours per day on their smart devices.[5]

Social media apps like Instagram and Snapchat (by the time you read this book those may be "out" and something else may be "in") pose multiple challenges for parents. First, they allow people to share photos or videos about whatever they want. Although Instagram officially has a "no nudity" policy, kids can use hashtags to easily find thousands of explicit images.[6] This does not count people posting "soft porn" images in their swimsuits or underwear. Snapchat allows users to post videos that can be seen by their followers but "disappear" in twenty-four hours. You can imagine what a kid might post if he or she is convinced it cannot be seen or retrieved by adults later.

Apps like Instagram, Snapchat, TikTok, and others also contain private messaging features that allow kids to post videos, chat, and communicate with one another. These private chat options evade most monitoring or filtering software that parents might have installed on devices. This ability for children and teens to be in constant, private communication with each other around the clock poses a major challenge for parents on a number of fronts:

---

[5] Ibid.

[6] "Instagram Has a No Nudity Policy, So Why Is There So Much Porn on the App?", Fight the New Drug (November 23, 2020), https://fightthenewdrug.org/if-instagram-strict-no-nudity-policy-but-still-porn/.

- To whom are our kids talking?
- Is their communication appropriate?
- Can we get their attention at home?
- Are they using their time wisely?
- Are they being lured into destructive temptations, relationships, and addictions that are too much for them to handle on their own?

Social media, smart devices, and internet technology have parents in a bind.

And of course, it's worth noting that this is *exactly* what social media companies want: attention and time. "Right now, the interests of parents are directly at odds with the interests of the technology companies. They're monetizing our attention and profiting off of our time. As they say, the addictive nature of smartphones is a feature, not a bug. We parents are outgunned and at a total loss."[7]

The Ubiquity of Pornography

As parents of boys, one of our biggest concerns about smart devices is pornography. When we give talks on parenting and technology, we always start by asking: "What are the chances our boys reach the age of eighteen without seeing any pornography?" The question elicits an awkward groan from the audience and

---

[7] Andrew Yang, "Our Kids Are Walking Around with Slot Machines in Their Pockets," Common Sense Media, https://www.commonsensemedia.org/our-kids-are-walking-around-with-slot-machines-in-their-pockets-andrew-yang.

they begin to answer out loud: "Zero." "No way." "Not going to happen." And they are probably correct. Studies show the average age of first exposure to pornography is eleven, while some say it's as early as eight years of age.[8] And it's not just a problem for boys. An estimated 93 percent of boys will be exposed to pornography before they are eighteen, but 63 percent of girls will too.[9] So the real issue isn't implementing a fail-safe "pornography protection plan"—nobody believes that's possible. Although we should still try to prevent exposure, our focus should be on creating a management plan that includes a redemptive response when kids sin or experience brokenness in this area. The combination of the internet, smart devices, and social media creates a seemingly endless minefield of temptation and potential exploitation for our kids.

The Negative Effects of Social Media and Smart Devices

Study after study shows that social media has negative mental health effects on kids and teenagers. There are some benefits to social media—expanded worldview, new and diverse friendships, instant communication, ability to speak out and stay informed on issues, etc. But Christian parents would be wise to be educated and engaged with potential pitfalls of this technology. They include:

---

[8] "What's the Average Age of a Child's First Exposure to Pornography?" Fight the New Drug (November 23, 2020), https://fightthenewdrug.org/real-average-age-of-first-exposure/.

[9] Ibid.

- **Peer pressure:** Social media creates pressure for kids to conform, whether that be pressure to post certain things or pressure to engage in unhealthy behaviors.

- **Unhealthy comparison:** Kids and teenagers work hard to create the perfect photos and selfies. They use a variety of lighting techniques, filters, and editing tricks to make themselves look better on their apps than they do in real life. These posed and edited pictures can contribute to a sense of inferiority and low self-esteem by both the subjects and the viewers of these posts.

- **Bullying:** Social media platforms are frequently used for kids to denigrate, threaten, or marginalize other kids. Parents should be watchful for bullying, whether our kids are the perpetrator or victim (at different times many kids end up being both).

- **Exploitation:** Social media apps and websites offer adults the opportunity to contact kids or teens using false identities. Kids often see themselves as more sophisticated or mature than they really are. This false confidence in their internet "street-smarts" gives cyber stalkers an opening to make contact and take advantage of minor children. Parents must educate our kids about these dangers.

- **Addiction:** The open secret of the tech industry is that social media apps and smart devices are literally designed to be addictive.[10] Most apps are "free" to the user, while the companies make money from advertising through the app. Many of these apps also mine your device for data and then use the data to sell more targeted and effective ads.[11] The app is built to compete ruthlessly for your attention. Designers have studied everything from dopamine releases in your brain (that's what kids get when someone "likes" a post), to attention spans, to aesthetics.[12] The entire experience of an app is created to gain and hold your attention for as long as possible.[13] The app designers also want you to return to the app frequently and habitually.[14] All of this stuff works—that's why children, teens, *and* adults spend hours each day scrolling through social media apps.[15] We are giving our private information and our time to technology

[10] Simon Fraser University. "Addictive De-vices: How We Can Unplug from this 21st Century Epidemic." *ScienceDaily* (October 3, 2019), www.sciencedaily.com/releases/2019/10/191003092039.htm (accessed November 14, 2020).

[11] Christopher Boyd, "How Social Media Platforms Mine Personal Data for Profit," Malwarebytes Labs (April 3, 2020), https://blog.malwarebytes.com/privacy-2/2020/04/how-social-media-mine-data-sell-personal-information-for-profit/.

[12] Virginia Smart and Tyana Grundig, "We're Designing Minds: Industry Insider Reveals Secrets of Addictive App Trade," CBC (November 3, 2017), https://www.cbc.ca/news/technology/marketplace-phones-1.4384876.

[13] Ibid.

[14] Ibid.

[15] Ibid.

companies. The addictive nature of social media makes technology management even more challenging for kids and parents.[16]

The addictive nature of social media makes technology management even more challenging for kids and parents.

God's Design for Technology

Christian parents need a biblical basis for talking about technology management. It is important to understand that God is not against technology. In the Bible, technological advances are generally seen as positive. Some examples include:

- Adam is instructed to "work" the garden, and that work presumably required him to develop tools (Gen. 2:15). That is technology.
- Cain's great-, great-, great-, great-, great-grandsons— one of whom played instruments and the other who forged metals—both used technology (Gen. 4:21–22).
- Noah is instructed to build an ark (Gen. 6:14ff). He certainly had to use tools and develop technology to accomplish *that* task.
- Joseph had a sophisticated inventory system (Gen. 41:19).
- Solomon created an engineering marvel (1 Chron. 28).

---

[16] "What Is Social Media Addiction?" Addiction Center, https://www.addictioncenter.com/drugs/social-media-addiction/.

- Nehemiah built the wall using men and women with multiple skills (Neh. 3).
- Jesus and the disciples used boats and fishing equipment (John 21).
- Paul used the Roman roads and postal system.[17]

It is the *misuse* of technology that causes problems. There are numerous examples in the Bible of the misuse of technology as well:

- There was the time a group of men set out to build a city to make a name for themselves, and God put a stop to it (Gen. 11:1–9).
- There were the Philistines who fashioned iron chariots and weapons to oppress Israelites, and God had to intervene to protect them (1 Sam. 13:5).
- King Nebuchadnezzar built a city for his own glory and God humbled him (Dan. 4:30).

Christian parents should not treat technology as inherently evil. Technology can be used for evil or for good. Our task is to manage technology in our families so that we maximize healthy connection and productivity while minimizing temptation and poor stewardship of time.

---

[17] Edwin M. Yamauchi, "On the Road with Paul: The Ease—and Dangers—of the Ancient World," *Christian History*, Issue 47, 17–18, https://christianhistoryinstitute.org/uploaded/50cf82181a7fd8.49814146.pdf.

Over time we want our children to see the dangers of technology for themselves so that they join us in actively managing its temptations. Ultimately, we want our adult children to take responsibility for their own management decisions and to be equipped to do so in a way that honors God.

"Core Sins" for Technology Management

A biblical framework for technology management requires the acknowledgment of sinful temptations offered by smart devices, social media apps, and the internet. While the possible sinful desires and actions related to technology are too numerous to catalog or predict, we have learned that there are a few "core sin" categories that will accurately address challenges our kids are having in this area. First John 2:16 is a classic Bible verse that helps us summarize and categorize temptation: "For the world offers only a craving for physical pleasure, a craving for everything we see, and pride in our achievements and possessions. These are not from the Father, but are from this world" (NLT).

In this one short Bible verse you can see the three basic categories of temptation: craving for physical pleasure, craving for everything we see, and pride in our achievements or possessions. If you were raised on the old King James Version, you have probably heard these referred to as the lust of the flesh, the lust of the eyes, and the pride of life. But how do these categories relate to technology?

Craving for Physical Pleasure

Sexual curiosity and sexual desire are normal parts of human growth and development. The internet offers innumerable opportunities for our children to get wrong information, subject themselves to destructive exposure, and open themselves up to dangerous habits and addictions. Because we are all sinners growing up in a fallen world, it is impossible for any of us to navigate our sexuality in complete sinlessness. We all struggle with lust and many of us have sinned sexually with our actions. Parents constantly have to discern whether their kids are exhibiting normal "growing up" curiosity and behavior or if kids are straying into more dangerous territory. But in conversations with our kids, parents need to be crystal clear that it is sinful to seek sexual stimulation or satisfaction outside of marriage.

When we find our kids struggling with internet-related sexual temptation or sexual sin, we need to be prepared for crucial conversations. These conversations are unlikely to be one-time events. All of these "little conversations" need to be part of the ongoing "big conversation" about sexuality that parents are always cultivating. Christian parents need to make sure our kids can get all the information and encouragement they need in the area of their sexuality from sound, wise, biblical sources. Our kids need to be constantly redirected to God's design for sexuality. And because of the availability of information on the internet, parents should start having these conversations with children at an early age.

We recently had a conversation with a mom whose eleven-year-old daughter had evaded parental controls, created multiple online identities, repeatedly viewed sexually explicit materials, and developed online friendships with strangers. In our conversation we discovered that the mom had not yet had "the" talk with her daughter. Of course, we encouraged the mom and gave her some suggestions for how to redemptively respond to the daughter's heart issues. We also encouraged her to be a bit more savvy in her technology management.

The point is that the mom was late. The internet beat her to the punch. The daughter was using the internet as her primary source to satisfy normal sexual curiosity. The mom's task is now to fight for her daughter's heart by regaining control of the sexual conversation. She has to introduce the truth and the beauty of God's design to combat the sin and brokenness that her daughter has been immersed in. The good news is that the little girl is a believer and her mom can remind her of the gospel. She is forgiven and the Holy Spirit can help her recover and pursue God's design. There is a lot of work ahead for this mom, but it can be done. Parenting is not for wimps!

Craving for Everything We See

As we noted earlier, the internet and social media are designed to gain and keep our attention. Younger people are particularly susceptible to the siren song of their smart devices. You can see this core sin manifested in raw screen time. Many young

Full Circle Parenting

people are convinced that if they aren't on their devices around the clock, they are missing out on meaningful social interaction.

We were literally in the middle of a writing session for this book when one of our kids called us upset. They had been to a high school party and other kids were using social media apps to take video and pictures of the various shenanigans taking place. Because our child isn't allowed to have social media apps on their phone, they felt like they were on the outside looking in. The other kids were instantly sharing and commenting on each other's posts. Then kids who weren't at the party were interacting with the posts as well. In the mind of the kids, the social media posts *about* the party were *at least* as important as the party itself.

> Many young people are convinced that if they aren't on their devices around the clock, they are missing out on meaningful social interaction.

This compulsion to post, like, comment, and receive online validation and feedback is a huge part of growing up for the current generation of young people. What do we as parents do about it? Here's what *we* did.

Mom: "I want to follow up on what happened at the party the other night." (Note: This conversation took place a few days after the actual incident; we needed to wait for things to emotionally cool down.)

104

Child: "Yes, I was so excited about the party and wanted to have a good time with my friends, but once I got there I was uncomfortable because I couldn't participate in everything they were doing and felt kind of left out. Once my 'friends' figured out I wouldn't pose for their snaps and wasn't posting on my own social media, they basically left me by myself. So I had nobody to hang out with. Those kids are so fake."

Mom: "I'm glad you are talking to us about this and I'm proud of you for choosing to do the right things. But let's be honest—are you saying that you were the only person there doing the right things and without social media?"

Child: "Well . . . no. There were other kids there that weren't doing it, but they weren't really . . ."

Mom: "Weren't really cool enough for you to hang out with? It seems like maybe you were trying to align yourself with the wrong people at the party. Maybe you should be more open to building friendships with a different group? It's hard enough to do the right thing—it can feel impossible to do it alone."

As you can see from this conversation, social media and technology aren't really the problem. They just highlight and locate and amplify the problem. The core sin here is a desire to find validation and significance from the wrong sources. Social media can dominate the thinking, interactions, and friendships our kids are experiencing. Parents need to constantly be engaged in helping kids recover and pursue God as the source of their self-image.

Keep reading for practical suggestions on monitoring and cultivating healthy screen habits. But Christian parents have to develop a strategy for talking about the core sin of craving everything we see. Social media causes kids to crave seeing— and knowing—everything. They want to know where everyone is, what everyone is doing, and what everyone is saying. This goes for celebrities and classmates. The craving extends to gaining knowledge and exposure that is not age-appropriate or parent-approved.

Christian parents have to be prepared to redirect kids to God's design, which is found in contentment and thinking of others. Young people also need to be encouraged to trust their parents and other God-given mentors to help them navigate a complex world of information and online relationships.

Pride in Our Achievements and Possessions

We all know what a "humblebrag" is and social media has allowed people to perfect it as an art form:

> "After 2 weeks of multiple health screens and asking everyone to quarantine, I surprised my closest inner circle with a trip to a private island where we could pretend things were normal just for a brief moment in time . . . I realize that for most people, this is something that is so far out of reach right now, so

in moments like these, I am humbly reminded of how privileged my life is." —@KimKardashian (Oct. 27, 2020)

"OH MY GOODNESS @GMC!!! I cannot wait to get my hands on one of these! Geesh . . . Brings back so many memories of my first Hummer . . ."
—@KingJames (Oct. 20, 2020)

"Totally walked down the wrong escalator at the airport from the flashes of the cameras . . . Go me."
—@joejonas (Dec. 30, 2010)

Of course, one of the benefits of social media is allowing friends and family to celebrate milestones with you. Special birthdays, anniversaries, and events are often announced and enjoyed by a network of friends around the country or around the world. But there is a fine line between appropriate sharing and narcissistic *over*sharing.

People of all ages constantly post selfies about their latest haircut, trip to the spa, vacation, tattoo, bathing suit, night out with their significant other, piece of furniture they refinished, birthday party they threw for their kids, or latest cooking experiment. This is why social media has created so much envy and resentment. People feel compelled to compete, to measure up, and to demonstrate competence and significance.

Why do we have this need to share with the world every detail of our lives? Every upgrade to our wardrobe? Every moment of leisure activity? Social media has made low-key narcissists of us all.

Young people are especially vulnerable to these temptations because they already lack judgment, maturity, and perspective. They will overshare, overinterpret, and overvalue the attention they get online. This core sin involves materialism, discontentment, greed, and covetousness. Watching others constantly brag and display their possessions or experiences online can create an unhealthy case of "the gimmes" (anybody remember the Berenstain Bears?). So how should Christian parents respond?

> Why do we have this need to share with the world every detail of our lives?

Parents should be intentional about recognizing sinful, prideful tendencies in ourselves and in our kids. The internet and social media do not create the sin—sin comes from our hearts. But social media magnifies and broadcasts our desire to be recognized as successful and important.

Christian parents should gently acknowledge sin and brokenness where they see it in their kids, but quickly pivot the conversation toward redemption. Our relationship with Jesus is what makes us significant. If our kids are believers, they need to hear again and again that God loved us, chose us, redeemed us, and forgave us. Because of the gospel we have the opportunity to truly change (that is repentance) our patterns of behavior and of seeking the wrong kind of validation through social media. With the help of parents, pastors, mentors, and counselors or therapists, our children can develop healthy ways of finding significance. Instead of using social media to magnify ourselves and our personal achievements, we can use it to highlight others, serve others, and draw attention to causes that are important in the world. The key is that parents should be prepared to create conversations that steer kids toward redemptive, positive heart-change. When the core sins of the heart are addressed, meaningful and lasting restoration becomes possible.

Practical Tips for Technology Management

I (Kristin) love history. My kids make fun of me because I light up at the thought of museums, biographies, and documentaries. I enjoy teaching our kids about men and women who have helped shape the world in which we live.

Winston Churchill was one of those men. Though absolutely flawed, he helped England avoid a German takeover during World War II. His speeches inspired his people to stay in the war, to keep fighting, and to realize that the enemy was brutal and unpacifiable. One of his speeches included these words: "We shall defend our island, whatever the cost may be, we shall fight on the beaches, we shall fight on the landing grounds, we shall fight on the field and in the streets, we shall fight in the hills, *we shall never surrender.*"[18]

---

[18] Winston Churchill, "We Shall Fight on the Beaches" (speech presented to the House of Commons, Westminster, England, June 4, 1940), International Churchill Society, https://winstonchurchill.org/resources/speeches/1940-the-finest-hour/we-shall-fight-on-the-beaches/.

These words inspired his nation. They inspire me as well. Parenting is a battle. We all feel that. Sometimes we get confused, though, about who the enemy is. We aren't in a battle with technology—technology has to be managed. We aren't in a battle with our children—our children have to be trained. God calls human beings to create and manage technology. That's part of what he meant when he commanded Adam and Eve to "have dominion" (Gen. 1:26 ESV). The enemy we face is the same enemy that every parent has faced since the fall.

Satan is the enemy. Peter called us to "Be sober-minded, be alert," because "Your adversary the devil is prowling around like a roaring lion, looking for anyone he can devour" (1 Pet. 5:8). The misuse of technology is one of his tools. He is brutal and unpacifiable. The use of technology can be for our good. It is the misuse of technology that is sinful and leads to brokenness.

Ever since the garden, Satan has tempted people to twist God's purposes and depart from God's design. Herein lies the battle. So as parents, we keep battling. We fight. We stand in the gap for our children and do our part to protect and train them. We don't give up. We don't sink into despair. We don't bury our heads in the sand. We don't surrender because it's too hard. Instead, we trust God, link arms with our church family, and take on the challenge.

So what are some practical ways parents can help kids manage technology?

Invade Their "Privacy"

As we said above, technology is always changing. New sites and apps spring up every day. A quick Google search will tell you that technology issues are a common parenting concern. There are articles from a myriad of sources outlining suggested best practices to implement, concerns to be aware of, and safeguards to put in place. Part of helping our children manage technology is taking the time to be aware of what is out there.

We can learn a lot by simply asking our children. They are experts in the area of technology. They know the latest apps, the coolest sites, and the most current tech trends. Have regular conversations with them about what they are seeing and experiencing online. We can't bury our heads in the sand on this issue.

Parents also have to be willing to invade the imaginary zone of privacy when it comes to technology. Moms and dads have the God-given authority to train the hearts of their children:

> "Love the LORD your God with all your heart, with all
> your soul, and with all your strength. These words
> that I am giving you today are to be in your heart.
> Repeat them to your children. Talk about them when
> you sit in your house and when you walk along the
> road, when you lie down and when you get up. Bind
> them as a sign on your hand and let them be a sym-
> bol on your forehead. Write them on the doorposts of
> your house and on your city gates." (Deut. 6:5–9)

Kids like to talk in terms of their privacy and their digital space. The truth is, kids don't have a private space. You are providing for them. Even if your kids work and pay for certain individual expenses, you are still creating the financial opportunity for them to do so. We tell our kids, "That's not your room, car, phone, shirt, etc. All of this belongs to Mom and Dad. We are just letting you borrow it."

> Parents who allow their children to feel a sense of ownership, privacy, and autonomy with no accountability are making a huge mistake.

On its face this may seem mean, but it's not. Parents who allow their children to feel a sense of ownership, privacy, and autonomy with no accountability are making a huge mistake. Their smart device is actually your smart device. You have the right and the responsibility to look at it whenever you choose. Kids are not prepared to manage unlimited freedoms, especially when it comes to technology.

No Tech in Private Spaces

One of the downsides of everyone having their own devices and their earbuds is that people retreat into their own "secret world" we talked about above. It isn't healthy for kids to have uninterrupted hours immersed online. We try to control access by limiting the places they are allowed to use their devices.

We have chosen to keep computers, cell phones, TVs, etc. in public family spaces while at home. We keep the childrens' rooms very simple. Their bedrooms are places to rest, read, and get dressed. We don't want them spending a lot of alone time in their rooms. We actually implemented this rule when our children were very young. It had little to do with managing technology and far more to do with our desire to foster a family-oriented environment. However, this idea does help us set healthy boundaries for our children.

Limit Screen Time

Another way to set healthy boundaries is to limit our kids' screen time overall. Research shows a direct correlation between increased screen time and increases in depression, suicide, and other mental health setbacks.[19] According to psychologist Jean Twenge in her book *iGen*, harmful effects kick in at two or more hours per day.[20] The negative impacts of comparison and constantly experiencing FOMO (Fear of Missing Out) have increased right along with the increase in social media availability. This has had a particularly negative impact on girls. "From 2010 to 2015, the percentage of teen boys who said they often felt left out increased from 21 to 27. For girls, the percentage jumped from 27 to 40."[21]

We need to do everything we can to guard our kids from the dangers of technology. When they were little, we taught them not

---

[19] Greg Lukianoff and Jonathan Haidt, *The Coddling of the American Mind* (New York: Penguin Books, 2018), 162.

[20] Jean M. Twenge, *iGen: Why Today's Super-Connected Kids Are Growing Up Less Rebellious, More Tolerant, Less Happy—And Completely Unprepared for Adulthood* (New York: Simon & Schuster, 2017).

[21] Lukianoff and Haidt, *The Coddling of the American Mind*, 154.

to stick their finger in the light socket or touch the stove. They may not recognize the dangers of too much screen time, but we have to do our best to protect them. We are asking too much of our kids if we give them unlimited access to technology.

Get Monitoring Software

Every computer and cell phone with internet access needs monitoring software. We know these aren't fail-safes, but it is our job to try. This is about boundaries and accountability. This isn't about catching our kids doing the wrong thing. We encourage you to be up-front about any software you install. Make sure your kids know that they are probably smarter than the software. You know if they want to, they can get around it. Still, this layer of protection is there to help them if they want to pursue the right things. Inevitably you will hear, "Don't you trust me?" President Ronald Reagan used to say, "Trust, but verify."[22] We trust them enough to give them certain freedoms, but we need to remind them that with those freedoms comes accountability.

Limit Internet and Social Media Access on Phones for Children and Young Teenagers

Contrary to what your child will tell you, every child does not need a cell phone. We encourage you to hold off as long as possible in providing one for them. If your family situation allows for your

---

[22] *Ronald Reagan*, Wikipedia, s.v. "Trust, but verify," accessed November 14, 2020, https://en.wikipedia.org/wiki/Trust,_but_verify.

child to operate without one, let them do so. Most of our older children did not get their first cell phone until they were fifteen or sixteen years old. However, our family situation may be different from yours. We're not trying to make a hard-and-fast rule. Some of our children were older than that, and some were younger. You will have to decide when your child needs a cell phone, and when they are old enough to handle the responsibility of it.

When you do decide to give them a phone, we suggest you consider limiting access to social media and the internet until they are mature enough to handle it. A cell phone is helpful in keeping track of your child and in giving them access to you when you are not physically there. However, those things can be accomplished without them having a smartphone with unrestricted internet access and every available social media app. If you choose to be more conservative than parents of your child's peer group, be prepared for constructive conversations with your kid and other parents. You're definitely going to feel the pressure to conform.

> If you're a Christian parent, you're going to have to be okay with swimming upstream.

If you're a Christian parent, you're going to have to be okay with swimming upstream. You can't let other people dictate how you parent or how you decide to help your child navigate these waters. Also be aware that pressure can go both ways. If you're the parent who gives your child a phone earlier, be considerate of parents around you who choose differently. The bottom line is that every child is different. You, as the parent, are responsible to make the best decisions for your tribe. Don't relinquish that responsibility to the child nor to those around you.

Be Careful with On-Demand and Live Streaming Programming

Movie night is a big deal in the Scroggins home. It always has been. We started it when our firstborn was about three years old. He turns twenty-five soon. That's a lot of movies. And because we have six sons, that's a lot of *Toy Story*, *Tarzan*, and *Remember the Titans* (and lots of gummy bears)!

Movie night has gotten increasingly difficult to navigate. When we started in 1999, we simply chose a VHS tape and watched it. Then we got fancy and moved to DVDs. Still, that was easy enough to manage. We only had the movies we purchased, and we only purchased the movies we wanted them to see.

Then, on-demand happened. It was awesome because of all of the choices we now had. It was also awful for the same reason. Then came Netflix, Hulu, Amazon Prime, YouTube TV, and more streaming options than we could keep track of. Now the movies that our younger children shouldn't even know about are ready and available at the click of a button.

These services do offer parental controls, which we appreciate and use. Still, how do we manage this ever-changing arena of technology? We need to have constant conversations about the importance of things we put in our minds and allow our eyes to see (Rom. 12:2; Matt. 6:22–23). These conversations will allow our kids to develop a grid for what is appropriate and acceptable for a Christ-follower to watch. They won't always be in our homes, but we must teach principles and give them tools to help them make these choices on their own.

Set Aside Device-Free Family Times

We were out to eat recently, and we noticed a family at a table sitting diagonally from us. They were a good-looking family—well dressed, well groomed, and well mannered. We noticed something else though. They didn't talk to each other—not a word. The son had his head buried in his cell phone with his ear buds in, engrossed in his screen. The parents just sat there and stared straight ahead. No one seemed mad. They were just in their own worlds.

It seems like we are raising a generation who is disengaged from those they love and immersed in a world of who they *wish* they could be. How sad. Don't do it, Mom and Dad. Fight for time together. Fight for meaningful conversations. Don't allow technology to rob you of quality interactions with your people. You have such a limited amount of time with them. Let's be intentional about making the most of it! Make eye contact with each other. Have a good time listening to each other. Encourage each other. Laugh together.

Meals are a great place to start. Gather all of the devices in one spot and leave them there. Friends of ours have a tray on their kitchen counter with a sign that says, "Great things happen when you put your devices down." This is a positive way to communicate to their children that family time is important. This is true at home and away from home. Consider leaving cell phones in the car when you go to a restaurant. Be creative. You know the best times to implement device-free living for your family. It does take intentionality. Our children aren't going to have this idea on their own. It's up to us as parents to make it happen.

Additionally, a pastor friend of ours, Tyler Core, recommends establishing a rhythm of fasting from social media: one day a week, one week a month, one week a year. Try something similar for yourself and your family.

Put Your Phone Down When Talking with Your Children

It really is up to us. We are the models. The idea that "kids have changed"—as if they just morphed into a new species on their own—is silly. Kids haven't changed on their own; we have changed them. Our expectations, interactions, teachings, and modeling have changed—which, in turn, has shifted them.

Our children have learned to love their devices because, if we're honest, they have seen us loving ours. We have to be the one to put our devices down. We have to initiate conversations with them. We have to look them in the eye when they talk to us. We need to be the ones to disengage from our devices and spend time with them. We don't want our children to think of us as people who loved checking Twitter, Instagram, and emails more than we loved being with them.

We do have work that must get done. We know that. We do everything from our devices—pay bills, schedule appointments, keep our calendars, return emails, keep up with loved ones, make to-do lists, set alarms, and more. We don't have to give our child our undivided attention every second of every moment that we're together. However, we must model setting aside our devices for major portions of our time together if we expect them to do the same.

A Sample Guide for Crucial Conversations

Mom: "I noticed you posted a lot on Instagram today. Do you think you're spending too much time doing that?"

Fifteen-year-old girl: "I don't think so. Why does it matter anyway? I'm not doing anything wrong. Besides, you're on your phone a lot too."

Mom: "Well, I believe that you aren't doing anything wrong in your mind. I'm just concerned that you may be allowing social media to influence the way that you think about things and dictate who you are and what you think is important. Let's talk about that."

Daughter: "Yes, but if I don't keep up with what's going on, I will look like a loser."

Mom: "I want you to feel good about your social standing. I know that's important. Could I help you think about that in a different way? God's design is for you to draw your identity from what he says about you. He also wants you to think about others and not yourself. When you post every detail of your life on social media, it indicates to me that you're searching for approval and recognition for the wrong reasons. You aren't going to be able to post enough, get enough likes, or get enough followers to feel good about yourself. Plus, I think you may be sending the wrong signals out about yourself. I want to help you do two things: regulate your screen time and help you think more carefully about the kinds of things you're posting. Let's come up with a game plan to help you going forward."

Like it or not, technology isn't going anywhere. This is—and will continue to be—a huge part of our kids' lives. The intentional conversations we have with them in this area are vital. We have to keep God's design in front of them. We want to lovingly address the sin and brokenness that inevitably come from the misuse of technology. We can continually remind them of God's redemptive plan to forgive and restore those who call out to him. As we do this, we guide them to the truth that they can hold to for all of life's challenges. No one besides us and our church family are telling our children these things. Keep telling them. Keep fighting for them. Keep leaning on your church family. Don't lose heart.

CHAPTER 5

Alcohol and Substance Abuse

Woe to those who rise early in the morning in pur-
suit of beer, who linger into the evening, inflamed by
wine. At their feasts they have lyre, harp, tambou-
rine, flute, and wine. They do not perceive the LORD'*s*
actions, and they do not see the work of his hands.
—Isaiah 5:11–12, the prophet Isaiah

South Florida, where we live, is called the "rehab capital" of the United States.[1] Hundreds of people in recovery attend our church each week. You could say that drugs and alcohol are just a part of the cultural landscape around here. It is probably the same to some degree wherever you live and raise your family. If you are

---

[1] Charlie Keegan, "What's in a Name? Is Delray Beach Really the 'Recovery Capital'?", wptv.com, April 20, 2017, https://www.wptv.com/news/region-s-palm-beach-county/delray-beach/whats-in-a-name-is-delray-beach-really-the-recovery-capital.

going to bring up children in this culture, you are going to have
to deal with the issue of alcohol and drugs.

Like cell phones, social media, and pornography, alcohol
and drug use are ubiquitous among young people. According
to research, 33 percent of teens between the ages of twelve and
twenty admitted to consuming alcohol in 2019.[2] Let's face it—
lots of kids drink. Lots of kids smoke pot. Lots of kids use all
kinds of drugs for fun, to be social, or as an escape. Even if your
kids don't—their friends will. And even if our kids aren't misusing alcohol or drugs today—70 percent of them will consume
alcohol and 50 percent of them will take illicit drugs at some
point in the future.[3]

As our kids have grown up, they have attended teenage parties from time to time. Some of these parties we knew about and
preapproved (especially when our kids were older high school-
ers). A few of these parties we were unaware of. I'm sure there
are things we are *still* in the dark about—and we are probably
better off for it! As it turns out, some of these get-togethers with
teenagers featured kids drinking and using drugs. We have been
surprised to discover that lots of kids are drinking or smoking
in public at these events even if parents are present and visible
at the party. To be clear—we are really proud of the choices our

[2] "2019 National Survey on Drug Use and Health," Substance Abuse
and Mental Health Services Administration of the U.S. Department of
Health and Human Services (September 11, 2020), https://www.sam-
hsa.gov/data/report/2019-nsduh-detailed-tables.
[3] Ibid.

kids have made in this area. Our kids aren't party animals, and as far as we know, they generally steer clear of trouble and leave events when they feel uncomfortable. But they are kids. And they live in this crazy world. And it's our job to help them pursue God's design.

One night one of our boys came home really upset. He had just graduated from high school and attended a "graduation bash" thrown by a school friend. At the party, one of his female friends got drunk—not too drunk to walk, but he felt that her judgment was definitely impaired. She ended up dancing and interacting with boys at the party in embarrassing ways. He tried to intervene and redirect his friend, but she was determined to "have a good time," and boys at the party were glad to oblige. He came home and said, "I can't believe what people will do when they drink too much. I can't believe that the guys at the party would treat her like that. I feel horrible for her because everyone at the party will always remember the things that went on tonight." Sad talk.

Throw teenage kids—even good kids—into challenging situations with peers, alcohol, sexual temptation, vehicles . . . you get the idea. This is the culture many of our kids are experiencing. As parents we aren't shocked, because it's not all that different from what was happening when we were their age (except for social media).

As parents, we need to answer some important questions:

- How can Christian parents prepare our kids for challenging environments?

- How can Christian parents teach our kids to make wise decisions about alcohol and drugs?
- How can Christian parents speak redemptively into the lives of our children if they make a mistake or develop a destructive habit?

We have to be prepared to point kids to God's design and his plan for restoration if a failure occurs.

Because of the pervasive use of alcohol in social situations, every parent is going to have crucial conversations with their children:

- Are we (the adults) going to normalize alcohol use in our homes? What about other legal drugs?
- Are parents going to encourage or discourage our kids to drink?
- How are we going to train our kids to deal with drinking and driving?
- Are we going to allow/encourage our kids to attend events where drinking and drug use is likely to occur?
- What do parents do when we become aware that someone else's kid is having drug- or alcohol-related problems?
- What about when one of our kids comes home drunk or high?
- What if one of our kids develops unhealthy patterns or addictions related to alcohol or drugs?

- On what basis will we have the above conversations? Does the Bible speak helpfully about God's design in this area?

Responsible parents need to be prepared in advance to deal with these types of questions and issues. Thankfully, the Bible gives us a lot of clear and helpful instruction so that we can help our children discover, pursue, and—if necessary—*recover* God's design for the use of alcohol and drugs.

God's Design: What Does the Bible Say?

Christian parents should point kids to Scripture as we seek to explain God's design for alcohol and drugs. The Bible has very little to say about recreational "drugs" other than alcohol, but the clear biblical principles dealing with alcohol can easily be applied to other substances. This section of the book is not intended to be an exhaustive discussion of biblical references to alcohol, but will instead try to help parents with a "Cliff's Notes" approach to the issue.

The Bible Does Have Positive Things to Say about Alcohol

According to the Bible, wine makes the heart happy (Ps. 104:15). Wine is seen as a blessing from the Lord (Gen. 27:28). Lack of wine is seen as a lack of blessing (Deut. 28:39). Many people in the Bible, including Jesus, drank wine responsibly and in a way that honored

God (Matt. 11:19). The first miracle of Jesus recorded in the New Testament was when he turned water into wine (John 2:1–11). Jesus gave wine to his disciples when he instituted the Lord's Supper (Luke 22:17–18). And Jesus will serve believers wine in heaven at an event called the marriage supper of the Lamb (Isa. 62:8–9). Paul noted that drugs can be medically beneficial and encouraged Timothy to use wine medicinally (1 Tim. 5:23).

Clearly, the Bible does not prohibit Christians from drinking alcohol. In many places Scripture seems to allow or even encourage it. Some anti-alcohol Christian preachers and scholars have attempted to argue that the alcohol used in the Bible was significantly less potent than what people drink in our society today and was more like slightly fermented "grape juice."[4] But this is not a strong or persuasive argument.[5] If the wine in the Bible is only slightly alcoholic, why the warnings about drunkenness (Eph. 5:18; Gal. 5:19–21)? If the wine Jesus made at the wedding was only "grape juice," then why was the host congratulated for saving the "good stuff" for last (John 2:10)? If the wine Jesus drank socially was not alcoholic, then why was he accused of "drinking with sinners" (Luke 7:34)?

---

[4] John MacArthur, "Beer, Bohemianism, and the True Christian Liberty," *Grace to You* (blog), August 9, 2011, https://www.gty.org/library/blog/B110809.

[5] S. Bacchiocchi, J. S. Blocker Jr., B. S. Easton, D. M. Edwards, J. A. Ewing, B. A. Rouse, J. F. Ross, R. S. Shore, J. M. Luce, and J. F. Sutherland, "Alcohol, Drinking of." In *Evangelical Dictionary of Theology*, edited by Walter A. Elwell (Grand Rapids, MI: Baker Academic, 2001), 41.

Some readers of this book may have deep, personal, religious, or cultural convictions or preferences prohibiting alcohol use. Full disclosure—we don't drink alcohol, and we don't have alcohol in our home. Many parents reading this drink socially and are able to do so responsibly. Many parents in our church drink alcohol, and do so in moderation. Whatever your personal situation, trying to tell intelligent children that the Bible prohibits drinking or that drinking is a sin is going to be a tough sell. Teaching our kids about God's design requires us to be clear and honest about what the Bible actually says. If our kids detect hypocrisy or dishonesty in our use of Scripture, they are unlikely to be persuaded by our conversations.

> If our kids detect hypocrisy or dishonesty in our use of Scripture, they are unlikely to be persuaded by our conversations.

Drunkenness and Addiction Are Sins that Lead to Deep Brokenness

One spring we took a family trip to San Francisco. Since our kids have all grown up in South Florida, San Francisco offered them a whole new set of experiences. The hills, the mild weather, the giant trees, and the spectacular city itself were all amazing. We spent one afternoon and evening at Fisherman's Wharf. There was music, great food, and beautiful views of the Golden Gate Bridge. As we walked together there were also lots of homeless people laying all over the sidewalks, many of them visibly drunk or high. These people were in various states of dress and undress—some were angry and profane and even threatening. Our younger children were quite shocked and a little bit unsettled. The deep brokenness that we saw on those streets was quite an object lesson about the consequences of sin—both personal and societal. That experience created a good opportunity to talk about all kinds of things, including the brokenness that can result from misusing drugs and alcohol.

While it is true that the Bible says some *positive* things about alcohol, the Bible also gives frequent and direct *warnings* about sins associated with drinking too much or being addicted to anything. Our society is well-versed on the personal and social costs of misusing drugs and alcohol. The financial burden is staggering, with a $600 billion price tag each year.[6] Forty-one billion dollars are spent annually on the war on drugs in America.[7] The rehab business is also a massive, multi-billion-dollar industry for a reason—a lot of people cannot, or will not, drink in moderation. Families, businesses, churches, and communities pay the price for

[6] "Principles of Drug Addiction Treatment: A Research-Based Guide" (3rd ed) National Institute on Drug Abuse," https://www.drugabuse.gov/publications/principles-drug-addiction-treatment-research-based-guide-third-edition/frequently-asked-questions/drug-addiction-treatment-worth-its-cost.

[7] "What America Spends on Drug Addictions," Addiction-Treatment.com, https://addiction-treatment.com/in-depth/what-america-spends-on-drug-addictions.

rampant drug and alcohol abuse in our culture. Nearly $437 billion a year is lost in business productivity alone.[8]

Christian parents will have a perspective that is unique. We aren't just trying to keep our kids from the *consequences* of sin—we are trying to help our kids pursue God's design for their lives. We actually care what the Bible says on the issue of alcohol. So, what does the Bible say about drunkenness?

The Bible gives Christians clear instructions not to get drunk. Ever. "And don't *get drunk* with wine, which leads to reckless living, but be filled by the Spirit" (Eph. 5:18, emphasis added).

The Bible teaches that drunkenness is a sin, and lumps drunkenness in with a bunch of other terrible sins. The Bible says that "drunkards" won't inherit the kingdom of God:

> Don't you know that the unrighteous will not inherit God's kingdom? Do not be deceived: No sexually immoral people, idolaters, adulterers, or males who have sex with males, no thieves, greedy people, *drunkards*, verbally abusive people, or swindlers will inherit God's kingdom. (1 Cor. 6:9–10, emphasis added)

The Bible says that drunkenness is a result of following our sinful nature:

> Now the works of the flesh are obvious: sexual immorality, moral impurity, promiscuity, idolatry,

---

[8] Ibid.

> sorcery, hatreds, strife, jealousy, outbursts of anger,
> selfish ambitions, dissensions, factions, envy, *drunken-*
> *ness, carousing,* and *anything similar.* I am warning you
> about these things—as I warned you before—that
> those who practice such things will not inherit the
> kingdom of God. (Gal. 5:19–21, emphasis added)

The Bible says that drunkenness is one of the "evil things that godless people enjoy." As Christians, these kinds of sinful activities may be part of our past, but they shouldn't be a part of our present or our future.

> You won't spend the rest of your lives chasing your
> own desires, but you will be anxious to do the will
> of God. You have had enough *in the past* of the evil
> things that godless people enjoy—their immorality
> and lust, their feasting and *drunkenness and wild par-*
> *ties,* and their terrible worship of idols. (1 Pet. 4:2–3
> NLT, emphasis added)

So while the Bible does not prohibit drinking in moderation, the Bible is very clear that drunkenness is prohibited for Christians. Parents should not hesitate to teach our kids what the Scriptures say—God's design definitely does not include getting drunk or high, and the sin of drunkenness can lead to all kinds of brokenness.

Alcohol and Substance Abuse Are Dangerous

When our family was walking down the streets in San Francisco, we could smell the stink of the drunks laying on the street. We had to avoid the discarded needles, broken bottles, feces, and urine that were scattered and splattered around the streets and walkways. The older boys and I (Jimmy) had to step between the girls and some of the men that were aggressive and profane with their comments and physical proximity. Of course, we understand that many of these people have had terrible lives. Some are veterans. Some are abuse victims. Some are mentally ill. All of them are created in God's image and are worthy of compassion and love. But on that day they provided a powerful visual illustration of the dangers and brokenness that can result from the misuse of drugs and alcohol. The patterns of physical, emotional, psychological, and spiritual brokenness we observed on the streets of San Francisco that day mirror the warnings about alcohol in the Bible.

- **The misuse of alcohol induces violence and leads unwise people astray.** Proverbs 20:1 says, "Wine is a mocker, beer is a brawler; whoever goes astray because of them is not wise." Roughly 40 percent of criminals incarcerated for violent crimes and convicted murderers admit to being under the influence of alcohol at the time of their offense.[9]

- **The misuse of alcohol leads to poverty.** Proverbs 23:21 says, "For the drunkard and the glutton will become poor, and grogginess will clothe them in rags." Thirty-eight percent of homeless individuals are dependent upon alcohol.[10]

- **The misuse of alcohol causes terrible judgment and can lead to addiction.** Proverbs 23:29–30 says, "Who has woe? Who has sorrow? Who has conflicts? Who has complaints? Who has wounds for no reason? Who has red eyes? Those who linger over wine; those who go looking for mixed wine."

- **The misuse of alcohol can lead people to drift away from God.** The prophet Isaiah wrote, "Woe to those who rise early in the morning in pursuit of beer, who linger into the evening, inflamed by wine. At their feasts they have lyre, harp, tambourine, flute, and wine. They do not perceive the LORD's actions, and they do not see the work of his hands" (Isa. 5:11–12).

---

[9] Carol Galbicsek, "Alcohol-Related Crimes," AlcoholRehabGuide. org, updated October 21, 2020, https://www.alcoholrehabguide.org/alcohol/crimes/.

[10] "The Connection Between Homelessness and Addiction," AddictionCenter.com, https://www.addictioncenter.com/addiction/homelessness/.

There is no doubt that all of these truths apply to substance abuse as well. Christian parents should take every opportunity to warn our children about the dangers of alcohol and substance abuse so that our kids can make wise decisions in this area of their lives. The choices they make can have far-reaching consequences for their families, their physical health, their finances, their reputations, and their relationship with God. While alcohol use is not prohibited in Scripture, the Bible is very pointed in its warnings about the dangers of drinking too much.

Believers in Jesus Should Not Be Addicted to Anything

As we have already noted, drug and alcohol addiction is a huge problem in our culture. Youth who start drinking at an early age are more likely to become addicted to alcohol at some point in their adult lives.[11] Every addict starts with a first time. Part of helping our kids pursue God's design is warning them to avoid the sin and brokenness of addiction. Scripture is crystal clear that Christians aren't supposed to be addicted or "mastered" by anything.

"Everything is permissible for me," but not everything is beneficial. "Everything is permissible for me," but I will not be mastered by anything" (1 Cor. 6:12). Paul's instructions in this verse ring true on the issue of drugs and alcohol. Even though

---

[11] Richard J. Bonnie and Mary Ellen O'Connell, eds., *Reducing Underage Drinking: A Collective Responsibility* (Washington: National Academies Press, 2004), https://www.nap.edu/read/10729/chapter/3#14.

the Bible does not prohibit drinking in moderation, this verse would encourage Christians to apply a cost-benefit analysis to lifestyle decisions and patterns. Just because something is permissible doesn't mean it is beneficial.

People with addictive personalities, genetic predispositions toward addictions, family history of addiction, or a poor personal track record of moderation would probably do better not to drink at all. Christian parents should have ongoing conversations with our kids about the dangers of addiction and the brokenness that comes along with it.

Leaders Should Be Really Careful with Alcohol

Every parent is a leader, and every Christian parent should be equipping their kids to lead as well. The book of Proverbs was written by Solomon—the wisest man in the world. Solomon was famous for his incredible accomplishments. He was a city planner, an architect, a builder, a poet, and a songwriter. And he was a wealthy and powerful king. By many measures Solomon was highly successful. But Solomon was not a very good dad. He made a lot of mistakes in the area of his family life.

When he got older, Solomon wrote the book of Proverbs, which is found in the Old Testament. Proverbs is written to Solomon's sons, presumably to help them become better dads than he was. Frequently in the book of Proverbs, Solomon warns his sons and grandsons about the pitfalls of misusing alcohol. As members of the royal family, Solomon wanted his kids to be effective national leaders. He was particularly concerned that alcohol would dilute or derail their leadership potential, and he detailed those concerns in the book of Proverbs.

- **Alcohol can be an attractive and seductive distraction for leaders.** Solomon warned, "Don't gaze at wine because it is red, because it gleams in the cup and goes down smoothly" (Prov. 23:31).
- **Alcohol can lead to laziness and poverty.** This is especially true if leaders surround themselves with drunks. Solomon's wisdom says, "Don't associate with those who drink too much wine or with those who gorge themselves on meat. For the drunkard and the glutton will become poor and grogginess will clothe them in rags" (Prov. 23:20–21).
- **Alcohol can cause leaders to exercise favoritism and poor judgment.** "It is not for kings, Lemuel, it is not for kings to drink wine or for rulers to desire beer. Otherwise, he will drink, forget what is decreed, and pervert justice for all the oppressed" (Prov. 31:4–5).

In addition to Proverbs, the Bible frequently and specifically warns *spiritual leaders* of the dangers of alcohol. For example, Nazarites were leaders in Israel that were specially committed and focused on spiritual things. Nazarites were forbidden from drinking alcohol (Num. 6:3). Levites were set apart to serve the Lord in the tabernacle and the temple. They were worship leaders. And they were instructed not to drink (Lev. 10:9). In the New Testament one of the qualifications for pastors of churches is that they shouldn't drink too much (1 Tim. 3:3). Isaiah notes that alcohol can cause religious leaders to lose spiritual vision (Isa. 28:7).

The Bible is clear that anyone who leads should be very careful with alcohol—it can cloud your judgment, incite violence, and lead to all sorts of terrible problems. Parents who choose to drink should make sure they do so in moderation. And Christian parents should create honest and clear conversations about God's design for alcohol and drugs, including appropriate warnings for aspiring leaders.

> Parents who choose to drink should make sure they do so in moderation.

We Are to Obey Civil Laws Regarding Alcohol and Drugs

Christian parents should instruct our children that God wants us to follow the civil laws as long as the civil laws don't violate our conscience or biblical convictions. There are federal, state, and local laws about drugs and alcohol, including rules addressing legal age, possession, distribution, and driving while intoxicated. To violate civil law in these matters is to violate God's design (Rom. 13:1–7). Parents absolutely should not facilitate underage drinking or drug use under any circumstance. To do so undercuts the authority of the Bible and surrenders the moral and ethical "high ground" from which parents instruct our kids. It is our responsibility as parents to teach our children the importance of following legal guidelines. Our obedience to these laws is actually obedience to God himself.

God Forgives and Restores Believers from the Sins of Drunkenness and Addiction

Because alcohol is such a fixture in our American culture, it is likely that many of our children will drink before they are of legal age. It is possible that you will discover one of your kids has been drinking regularly, or even has developed a serious addiction. Perhaps you will catch them, or maybe they will come to you and confess it. Either way, Christian parents must be prepared to have redemptive conversations with our kids about alcohol and drug use.

> Believing parents need to be prepared to forgive and restore.

Whether your child has made a "one-time mistake" or engaged in a pattern of sinful behavior, Christian parents must remember our theology. Our kids are sinners and our kids are complex. But God is a forgiver and a restorer, and believing parents need to be prepared to forgive and restore.

Paul noted that many Christians have challenges with alcohol in their past. After making a list of the sordid sins many believers used to struggle with, he wrote: "And some of you used to be like this. But you were washed, you were sanctified, you were justified in the name of the Lord Jesus Christ and by the Spirit of our God" (1 Cor. 6:11).

As parents, we need to keep in mind that God delights in restoring and renewing us from our brokenness. Jesus came to wash us clean from our sins and he has made us right with God through his cross and resurrection. When our kids mess up, we simply need to remind them of the gospel, and help them recover and pursue God's design again.

Kids don't need parents to judge them or constantly remind them of their shortcomings—they probably already feel bad enough. Kids need parents to love them and call them to repentance. We need to forgive them and lovingly walk them back toward God's design. We know that this is easier said than done. If our kids become addicted, we will likely need the help of professionals, and we will have to commit to walking the long road of recovery with them. While we haven't experienced this with our own kids to this point, we have walked alongside many, many people who have dealt with—and are dealing with—addiction. It isn't easy. This is why parenting isn't for wimps. This is why we can't go at it alone. Christian parents have the Bible, the Holy Spirit, and our church family to help us make our way forward. We have to choose daily to trust the Lord and stay in the game with our kids. We have to be prepared to take it one crucial conversation at a time.

Talking to Kids about Alcohol and Substance Abuse

Make Sure Kids Know the Facts about Alcohol and Drugs

Television commercials, movies, and social media are not in the business of telling our kids the truth about drugs and alcohol.

They often make drinking and drug use look glamorous and chic. There are lots of social media posts of people drinking with their buddies but very few about what happens after the parties are over. You never see someone posting about their DUI. Rarely do you see a commercial about someone with a hangover or regretting decisions they made while under the influence.

Tell your kids the truth about alcohol and drugs. Inform them about the facts. We would encourage you to have these conversations earlier rather than later. Let them process the information before they have to do something with it. Help them think through situations before they are faced with them. The National Institute on Alcohol Abuse and Alcoholism has some great resources to help parents have these conversations. They advocate for all of the above and give other practical tips.

Consider Family History

The Scroggins family gets obsessed with things quickly and naturally. We are college football nuts and obsess over our teams. We play a handful of the same board games over and over. We eat the same meals on a constant rotation. We drink sodas by the cases and eat gummies by the truckload. (Don't worry, we eat fruits and vegetables too.) The point is, we tend to get obsessed with things quickly and easily and we seem to enjoy it that way.

Actually, the tendency to obsess is in our DNA. Both sides of our family have people with addictive personalities. We have multiple family members who have become alcoholics or gotten involved with drugs. We have had a front-row seat to the effects of alcoholism: it wrecks marriages, derails careers, and ruins relationships. Family history is real. We all are predisposed to certain actions and desires, and we inherit sinful tendencies from our parents. The Bible talks about how the "sins of the fathers" are "visited" on the children for multiple generations. Children are not *guilty* of the sins of their parents or grandparents. But children do tend to follow the sinful *patterns* of previous generations in their families. Christian parents should make our kids aware of family history.

> Children are not *guilty* of the sins of their parents or grandparents. But children do tend to follow the sinful *patterns* of previous generations in their families.

Both Jimmy and I (Kristin) have heard the stories of foolish decisions and family heartache that were facilitated by alcohol. That's why our parents encouraged us not to be drinkers. One thing is for sure: If you don't drink, you will never get drunk. If you don't drink, you will never become an alcoholic. The same goes for any kind of substance abuse. "I think I'll become an alcoholic or drug addict" . . . said no one ever. Addiction is so subtle and seductive, at least at first. People become enslaved and can't find the way out. Parents should do everything we can to appropriately warn and inform our kids about the history of alcohol and drugs in our families.

Be Aware That What You Do in Moderation, Your Kids Tend to Do in Excess

Wouldn't it be a relief if we could just dabble in guilty pleasures without any negative effects on our children? We have eight kids, and we can tell you that we can never eat a piece of chocolate or have a bowl of ice cream in peace. The minute one of us goes for it everyone else piles on. Our children observe what we do and see what's important to us. Not only do they notice, they tend to join in.

As parents, we have to consider our influence as we make lifestyle choices about alcohol consumption in our homes, at other people's homes, and when we're out to dinner. We may be able to handle it, but what if our kids can't? What if they watch what we do in moderation and choose to do it in excess? It's our job as parents to abstain from behaviors that could lead our kids to stumble. The Bible actually talks about this. God tells us to look out for those who are "weak in faith" (Rom. 14:1). Paul wrote, "It is a good thing not to eat meat, or drink wine, or do anything that makes your brother or sister stumble" (Rom. 14:21). As parents, we need to take this principle to heart.

Help Your Kids Navigate Peer Pressure

"When we go to church today, people are going to say hello to you. Remember to look them in the eye, smile, and say 'hi.' We can be kind, even if we are shy." This is a conversation we had with our four-year-old daughter almost every single Sunday morning. She was nervous around people and would freeze up when they spoke to her. She would get uncomfortable and just ignore them. Obviously, her response wasn't acceptable, but putting her on the spot by correcting her in the moment was not a recipe for success. This is why we practiced at home. We would either have quick conversations about the importance of being polite or take the time to role-play with her. We wanted to help her get ready to greet those she came into contact with.

After a while, it worked! Conversations got more natural for her. In fact, she learned to initiate interaction with others and became quite the conversationalist. What's the point? The point is, you should prepare ahead of time.

We recognize that our younger children are constantly encountering new situations that require training and guidance. We also know that they handle situations better if they are prepared ahead of time. It's easy and natural to role-play with a four-year-old but what about our fourteen-year-old? Teenagers seldom make great choices in the midst of powerful temptation. Teens and preteens are dealing with new situations every day and some may catch them off guard. As parents we want to help them think through possible scenarios that may arise. This is what our parents did for us. My (Kristin) dad's words still ring in my ears: "Decide what you are going to do before you get there." Parents should constantly remind our kids to decide how they are going to handle a situation before the situation is upon them.

Your child will encounter a situation at some point that goes a different direction than they anticipated it would go. They may be at a party that they thought would be a good environment, but everything goes south. Someone shows up with alcohol or drugs. Now what do they do? Help your teenager build a mental "tool kit" of ways to handle those moments. Help them develop "scripts"—ways they could excuse themselves without completely losing face. A "script" would be something like: "Sorry, guys, but my dad wanted me to come home early tonight." Or, "My brother needs the car, so I have to head home." We have given our teenagers total freedom to throw us under the bus anytime they want. They can easily use us as an excuse if they need a reason to leave.

Children of all ages need to be "scripted," and role-playing is an effective parenting technique. Simply have your child practice their scripts with you before they leave so they are ready for any eventuality.

Remind Your Kids That God Has a Plan for Them

Proverbs 22:1 has become our family verse: "A good name is to be chosen over great wealth; favor is better than silver and gold." We want our children to remember when they are away from home, they represent the Scroggins family. Even more importantly, they represent the family of God. Alcohol and drugs are often used by the enemy to derail the plans God has for children. Why do you think the Bible contrasts getting drunk with wine with being filled by the Holy Spirit (Eph. 5:18)?

In the 3 Circles conversation diagram, we use squiggly lines to represent attempts to alleviate or escape brokenness. When we talk with our kids about brokenness, we point out various ways people deal with their brokenness. People often choose to make alcohol or drugs one of those "squiggly lines." Maybe they are

 looking for an escape, or to numb the pain. But they don't realize these paths only lead to deeper, longer lasting brokenness. We want to help our kids avoid these paths at all costs.

As Christian parents, we have to continually remind our kids that the only way to escape the brokenness of sin is through the gospel. We want to continually put God's design in the forefront of our children's minds. Our conversations should be centered around God's design for them, the brokenness they experience when they depart from his design, and the restoration that can be theirs as they repent and believe in his plans and purposes for them. Conversations focused on these truths are so much more effective than speeches focusing on behavior ("don't do this or that") or encouraging deception ("if I catch you doing that . . ."). Instead, Christian parents should give our kids "the why" behind the truths we are teaching them. God's design is the why.

Be Redemptive

God never gives up on us. The Bible says, "A person's steps are established by the LORD, and he takes pleasure in his way. Though he falls, he will not be overwhelmed, because the LORD supports him with his hand" (Ps. 37:23–24). These verses comfort us as people and as parents. They embody the idea of redemption.

The Lord will not allow us to be permanently ruined if we repent. God will redeem. God will restore. God holds out his hand to help us recover and pursue his design. Our children need to hear the possibility of redemption and restoration.

Our kids' actions do not define them. We must talk to them in these terms. If you find yourself dealing with a child who has gone somewhere you told them not to go, if they come home drunk, if you find drugs in their backpack, if you are concerned about who they are hanging around, remind yourself of the gospel. If they are believers, then they belong to God. Our parenting conversations should reinforce God's unwavering love for them.

A Sample Guide for Crucial Conversations

Son: "I'd like to go to a party my teammate is having this weekend."

Dad: "Okay. Tell me what you know about the party."

Son: "It's at his house. His parents will be home. It's just some guys and girls in our class getting together. We will probably just eat and hang out."

Dad: "Sounds fun. Do you feel good about the group of people that will be there?"

Son: "I do. They aren't all Christians, if that's what you mean. But they are good kids."

Dad: "I'm fine with you going if you feel good about it, but what is your plan if things start happening that you don't want to be a part of?"

Son: "Well, I know I should just leave, but I don't want to look like a nerd, or like I'm judging them."

Dad: "I get that. Let's agree that if things go sideways, you can just bow out gracefully. What could you say that would let you leave without making a huge deal about why?"

Son: "I could say, 'Guys, I think I'm going to head out. I've got an early morning tomorrow.'"

Dad: "Great! Sounds like a good plan."

This seems like such a simplistic conversation. It is. You could probably come up with better wording or some better "outs." The point is, we need to have conversations with our children that help them prepare for the "what ifs" of life. They *will* be exposed to drugs and alcohol. They *will* find themselves in situations they shouldn't be in. It is our job as parents to help them manage these situations in a way that holds true to God's design. We cannot choose their responses for them, but we can show them what it looks like to live a life with God's design at the center.

CHAPTER 6

Bitterness, Forgiveness, and Restoration

Forgiveness is not an occasional act;
it is a permanent attitude.[1]
—Martin Luther King Jr.

People get hurt. People get sad and mad. People get bitter. It happens to adults. It happens to kids. It's happened to us and it's happened in our family. It's tough stuff, requiring tough conversations. But they are conversations parents need to be prepared to have.

---

[1] Martin Luther King Jr., *The Papers of Martin Luther King, Jr. Volume VI: Advocate of the Social Gospel September 1948–March 1963,* ed. Tenisha Hart Armstrong, Clayborne Carson, Susan Englander, Susan Carson, Troy Jackson, and Gerald L. Smith (Los Angeles: University of California Press, 2007), 448.

We'll never forget the anger in his eyes. It was anger mixed with hurt—deep, sad, gut-wrenching hurt. Our son looked at us and said, "I will never trust [brother] ever again. He's a liar. And he only cares about himself." And then came the tears. As we watched our son try to "man up" and swallow his sobs, we knew that he needed help thinking through his feelings and his response to his brother's sins against him. This was a crucial moment, because he was going to have to choose between forgiveness or bitterness, closeness or distance, love or apathetic detachment.

His brother was a mess, at least for a while. He had our family totally disoriented. The brother had been doing things he shouldn't have done, taking things that didn't belong to him, and going places he was prohibited from going. Then he was lying about it, and getting his siblings to cover for him. The son with the tears had had enough. He had stuck up for his brother, stuck up for his brother's reputation, and had nearly come to blows at school when other kids accused his brother of all kinds of sinful behavior. He told his brother's accusers, "He didn't do that stuff. He told me he didn't do it. You don't know what you are talking about. You better shut your mouth about my brother or I'll shut it for you." Only he found out later that his brother *had* done the stuff. And then he lied to his siblings and let them stick up for him. Eventually the lies were exposed, the brother repented and asked for forgiveness, and the siblings were all willing to forgive and move on. All except this one son. He had put skin in the game for his brother, and he wasn't having it.

All of us have been there one way or another. We have all been hurt. And it is natural to want to make the ones that hurt us hurt the way that we hurt. That's why the old cliche "hurt people hurt people" is true. As parents we are going to see our kids get hurt. People will do them wrong. They will be overlooked, made fun of, and put down. These put-downs can be especially harmful if our kids are mocked for physical characteristics that they can't easily change such as physical deformities or blemishes, disabilities, lack of athletic or academic ability, etc. And when kids feel betrayed by people they believed were trustworthy—watch out! Betrayal breeds bitterness. As they grow up, our children will be tempted to become bitter against their peers, parents, siblings, and others.

Fortunately for us, our son was able to forgive his brother. It took time and lots of conversations. The offending brother eventually went through a period of deep repentance and did the work to rebuild trust with his brothers and sisters. That period of rebellion and bitterness is in the distant past. But restoration was only possible because we reminded all the involved parties about the gospel. As forgiven people, we have to forgive others (Eph. 4:32). And while forgiveness doesn't erase our brokenness, it does allow the hurt to heal. Forgiveness allowed us to recover and pursue God's design for love, unity, and peace in our family.

Parents must be prepared to have conversations with our kids about bitterness. Bitterness has to be addressed and defused. The longer it goes the deeper it gets. Bitterness can ruin a kid's disposition, their emotional health, and relationships. A child who develops the habit of giving in to bitterness at a young age can create patterns of negativity, discontentment, and ugliness that persist into adulthood. So as parents we have to be prepared to deal with comments like the following:

- "The kids at school said I'm stupid. I hate them."
- "My girlfriend cheated on me. She's trash."
- "My teacher treated me unfairly. She's a racist."
- "My youth pastor plays favorites. He's a hypocrite."
- "My brother lied to me. I'll never trust him again."
- "You guys got divorced. You are so full of it."

The good news is that God has a design for dealing with hurt. The Bible is full of instructions about how to treat those who mistreat us. Forgiveness is not the easy answer, but it is always the right answer. Wise parents will teach their children why and how to forgive. Wise parents will teach their children why and how to seek forgiveness. If we can teach our kids to let go of bitterness and pursue restoration, we will give them a priceless gift.

God's Design for Dealing with Bitterness

Bitterness Is Real

The Bible talks frequently about the problem of bitterness in both the Old and New Testaments:

- Proverbs acknowledges the reality of bitterness (Prov. 14:10).
- Ecclesiastes warns of the foolishness of bitterness (Eccles. 7:9).
- James encourages believers to deal honestly with bitter feelings (James 3:14).
- Hebrews tells us bitterness can defile you (Heb. 12:14–15).
- Ephesians tells us to get rid of bitterness (Eph. 4:31).

When parents observe our child experiencing emotional hurt, we need to be aware that the hurt can lead to bitterness. Of course the child might have serious anger against the person that hurt them. Anger isn't always wrong—it may be completely justified. Anger against injustice, unkindness, or meanness can be a good thing. Righteous anger can motivate us to stand up against bullies of all kinds.

Parents don't need to treat justified anger as if the anger itself is wrong. Scripture says to "be angry and do not sin" (Eph. 4:26a). But that anger needs to be dealt with in the right way. That's why the Bible also says, "Don't let the sun go down on your anger" (Eph. 4:26b). The Bible warns us that anger can grow into a "root of bitterness" (Heb. 12:15)—in other words, the anger can begin to control us if we let it. Righteous anger needs to be channeled into action. What can actually be done to right the wrong? Bring justice to the situation? Or bring reconciliation to the broken relationship? Wise parents will give their children the help and direction they need to work through anger.

Christian parents must help our kids avoid the pain and futility of bitterness.

Forgiveness Is the Antidote to Bitterness

Even if righteous anger has no viable outlet. Even if the one who has hurt us is going to get away with no repercussions. Even if there is no possibility of receiving an apology or any restitution. The right, healthy, and best course of action is for our children to choose forgiveness. We can help them get there. It's not always easy because when our kids are hurt, we may feel hurt. When our kids are angry, we may feel angry. When our kids are disappointed, we may feel disappointed. As parents we may be processing our own bitterness. This dynamic allows Christian moms and dads to show them the way.

Forgiveness alone enables you to let go of grievances, grudges, rancor, and resentment. It's the single most potent antidote for the venomous desire for retributive justice poisoning your system.[2]

Forgiven People Forgive People

Just like hurt people hurt people—forgiven people should forgive people. Christian parents have to drive this concept home with our kids. When they experience brokenness because of injustice, unfairness, bullying, racism, rudeness, or meanness (and they will), we must point them to the gospel. The gospel of

---

[2] Ibid.

Jesus gives our kids the platform and the power to forgive others. They can forgive even when the antagonists don't deserve it, don't want it, and don't think they need it. Crucial conversations about bitterness should include the following ideas:

- **We are all sinners** (Rom. 3:10–12, 23). Even though this parenting conversation is precipitated by someone sinning against our child, parents have to gently remind our kids that they are sinners too. They may not have sinned in *this* situation, but they definitely sin in *other* situations.

- **We all owe a "sin debt" of death to God because we have violated his design for our lives** (Rom. 6:23). Our kids need to be reminded that however badly we have been hurt by the sins of others against us, we have hurt our relationship with God by our own sins against him.

- **Jesus cancelled our "sin debt" on the cross** (Col. 2:13–15). Jesus has cancelled our sins by paying our debt when he was crucified in our place. When we became Christians, we were forgiven for all of our sins, even though we didn't deserve it.

- **Jesus requires forgiven people to forgive people.** We find this command in the Sermon on the Mount (Matt. 6:14) and the Lord's Prayer (Matt. 6:12). It is hypocritical for us to claim undeserved forgiveness from Jesus and then refuse to extend it to others. Jesus told a whole story to illustrate this principle that is often called the Parable of the Unforgiving Servant (Matt. 18:21–35). In this story, Jesus rebukes the forgiven person who refuses to forgive others.

The bottom line is that for Christians, forgiveness is not optional. We have to do it even when it is painful. Parents can remind hurt or angry children that when we forgive others, we imitate Jesus. We are never more like Jesus than when we forgive others. Parents should emphasize that forgiveness doesn't always come naturally—it is a choice. The Holy Spirit is there to help us do what we could not do in our own strength. Forgiven people must forgive people.

> For Christians, forgiveness is not optional.

Forgiveness Defined

So, what is forgiveness? Forgiveness is choosing to live peacefully with the consequences of another person's sin. We are going to have to live with the consequences anyway, whether we get an apology or restitution or not, so we might as well do it without the negative spiritual, emotional, psychological, and physical effects of bitterness in our hearts.

In addition to living with the consequences, forgiveness means that we choose to release our right for retribution to God. The effect of releasing the offender to God is to release ourselves from the compulsion to strike back, to make them hurt like we have been hurt, or to take revenge. Romans 12:16–19 gives clear instructions on this:

> Live in harmony with one another. Do not be proud;
> instead, associate with the humble. Do not be wise in
> your own estimation. Do not repay anyone evil for
> evil. Give careful thought to do what is honorable
> in everyone's eyes. If possible, as far as it depends
> on you, live at peace with everyone. Friends, do not
> avenge yourselves; instead, leave room for God's
> wrath, because it is written, "Vengeance belongs to
> me; I will repay," says the Lord.

These twin components of biblical forgiveness are powerful and effective in terms of our relationships with those who have hurt us. When we forgive, we choose to live with the consequences of their sin and release them to God. If our children can learn to truly forgive, they will be able to live lives that are free from the bondage of bitterness. These are parenting conversations worth having.

What Forgiveness Doesn't Mean

There is quite a bit of misinformation among Christians about forgiveness, what it requires, and how it works. Christian parents will help our kids choose forgiveness if we clarify what the Bible actually requires them to do. We can help our kids understand:

- **Forgiveness doesn't mean forgetting.** We've all heard the cliche "forgive and forget." If someone means by that statement that we should forgive people and move on with our lives, then fine. But the idea that we're literally going to forget is incorrect. You can choose to forgive, but you cannot choose to forget. Your son or daughter can't invoke voluntary, selective amnesia about someone who has hurt them. And they shouldn't.

- **Forgiveness doesn't mean remaining vulnerable.** When someone hurts you or betrays you, they are signaling that they are not worthy of trust. They might be able to regain your trust, but forgiveness doesn't require you to trust them again. If someone is violent or predatory, you can forgive them (live peacefully with consequences and release them to God), but you don't have to give them opportunities to hurt you again. You can forgive without being friends with them again. You can forgive without liking them again. And you can forgive without allowing yourself to be in physical or emotional proximity to them again. Different situations call for different levels of physical or emotional distance. You can forgive and still protect yourself. Our kids need to understand these truths.

- **Forgiveness doesn't mean releasing the offender from any consequences.** For example, if someone commits a crime against your child, the offender should face repercussions. Your child may choose to forgive the person, but if the opportunity exists to receive restitution, it is not wrong to take it. Releasing the person to God doesn't mean you don't tell the school official, the parent, or the police officer what happened. Releasing the person to God doesn't mean shielding them from social, relational, financial, or legal ramifications of their actions.

- **Forgiveness doesn't mean God is letting them off the hook.** Forgiveness actually means believing God's justice is better than our justice. When we are hurt, it is normal to daydream about what consequences we would like to pour out on our offender. Our kids will have the same feelings and thoughts. They might want to punch them in the face, embarrass them, or socially destroy them. They may have the urge to physically injure or even "kill" them. These are the kinds of things that people think about when we are hurt. Forgiveness is difficult because it means releasing the retribution to God. If we are honest, we are afraid that God's justice won't be as painful to our offender as our "justice" would be. But this is foolishness. Think about what God's justice demanded of Jesus in order to obtain our forgiveness—the cross. Is your justice more violent than the cross? Think about what God's justice demands of people who are not forgiven by Jesus—eternal hell. Is your justice more painful or long-lasting than hell? God is a righteous judge. He is able to weigh all relevant factors—motives, opportunities, circumstances—all because he can see things we can't see. Our children can be confident that when they release someone to God, his justice is up to the task. God's justice should encourage our kids to be forgivers.

- **Forgiveness doesn't require an apology.** Many times people who hurt us are not sorry for what they have done. They may not think that what they did was wrong. They may not care. They may not even know we've been hurt. It has been said that bitterness is like drinking poison and then hoping it hurts the other person. Forgiving others allows us to gain freedom from bitterness without requiring *anything* from the person who hurt us. We simply choose to forgive them in our hearts, even if they don't ask for it, want it, deserve it, or agree that they need it. If our kids are waiting for an apology before they forgive, then the offender is still in control. The one who hurt them in the first place is continuing to hurt them by filling them with bitterness. Forgiveness releases our kids from the offender's control, and allows our children to move forward with peaceful hearts.

God's justice should encourage our kids to be forgivers.

- **Forgiveness doesn't require a cathartic conversation.** Some people say that in order to forgive you have to "face your offender." But that's just not true. When the offender doesn't agree that they are wrong, or if they don't care, it is futile to try to *confront them* with their sin so you can *forgive them* for their sin. Confrontations like that are likely to escalate tension and cause even more problems. Of course there are certain relationships where it might be appropriate to say, "When you said this or did that, it really hurt me." But that conversation presumes the person is ignorant of the offense and would want to make things right. In many situations where our kids are hurt, the best thing to do is simply choose to forgive. The truth is your child can forgive the offender without the offender ever knowing it. The offender's participation in the forgiveness process isn't really necessary. We can just forgive them—that's it!

Forgiveness Is Both an Event and a Process

Forgiveness is a choice. It is not an emotion or a feeling. Forgiveness—living peacefully with consequences and releasing the offender to God—is something an individual has to choose for themselves. Parents can't choose forgiveness on behalf of our kids, but parents can train our kids to choose the relief and freedom that come from forgiving others. Forgiveness starts with a choice at a moment in time—"I am choosing to forgive this person, right now." So forgiveness is an event. That is one of the goals of these parenting conversations—to persuade and train our kids to choose to forgive others.

The problem is that after our kids have made this choice, they are still likely to struggle with feelings of hurt, anger, and bitterness. This is normal. This isn't unspiritual. This isn't a sign that the choice to forgive was a lie. The choice to forgive doesn't erase the painful memories, the hurt, or the consequences that our kids have to live with. Some hurts require multiple parenting conversations. Some hurts may call for conversations with a pastor or church mentor or therapist. Whatever the case, parents should not be surprised if those memories and feelings come back up for months or even years. There are some hurts that last a lifetime. This is why forgiveness is also a process.

What do we tell our kids to do when those hurt feelings resurface? Our kids need to constantly remind themselves of the gospel of Jesus and choose to forgive their offenders all over again. Rinse. Repeat. For the rest of their lives, if necessary. Over time it is likely that the bitter feelings will recede, and the forgiveness will feel more solid and permanent. But that result is not guaranteed. Forgiveness is an event, but forgiveness is also a process. Parents need to train our kids to lean on the power of the Holy Spirit, the support of their church family, and the love of their parents to continually make the choice to forgive.

Restoration Is the Goal

In the best-case scenario, the person who hurts our kids will repent and apologize. When they sense genuine repentance, it is easier to forgive. And when repentance is coupled with forgiveness, the result is restoration. Full restoration isn't always possible or desirable, but within a family or between fellow Christians restoration and reconciliation is the ultimate goal. We need to encourage our kids toward this end.

Of course, there are many times when our kids will need to forgive people who are not repenting and will not apologize. What does restoration look like in those situations? For a variety of reasons, restoration of the human relationship may not always be achievable. But bitterness affects more than just our relationships with other people. Let's not forget that bitterness is sinful. Bitterness creates internal brokenness in the hearts of our children, and bitterness also creates brokenness in the relationship between our kids and God. When our kids choose to engage in the process of forgiveness, they will begin to experience an increasing sense of internal peace. That's restoration. They will also have a sense of holy satisfaction that comes from lining up with God's design. That's restoration too.

One of our grandchildren was born with a broken collarbone. Fortunately, most babies are born with an amazing ability to heal. Within a week the bone had fused itself back together. But a big scary knot appeared where the break was healing. After a while, the knot went away and it looked normal. The doctor said the bone would actually be stronger after it healed than it was before. Forgiveness can work like that in a relationship. The damage is real, but forgiveness facilitates healing. After a while the relationship can actually be stronger than it was before the brokenness. Bitterness and anger make us *feel* strong—that's a mirage. But forgiveness and restoration actually *make us* strong—that's God's design.

Talking to Kids about Bitterness, Forgiveness, and Restoration

Anybody reading this have a long memory? I (Jimmy) do. There is definitely a part of me that likes to hold a grudge. I secretly appreciate bumper stickers that say, "I don't get mad . . . I get even." In times when getting even is impossible, I still tend to fantasize about it. I think about what it would be like if the person who hurt me could hurt at least as much as I hurt. Even better if they could be hurt in public. That way they could be humiliated while they hurt.

Maybe you are thinking: *What is this guy doing writing a parenting book? He needs counseling!* True enough. But maybe some of you parents know how the temptation of bitterness feels. Maybe you have laid awake at night thinking about what you would like to happen to your boss or your ex or that friend who let you down. I guarantee you some of our kids feel the same way from time to time.

I (Jimmy) remember when I was in the tenth grade and my dad got fired. He was the football coach at my high school and I was on the team. I was embarrassed for him and for me. I had to listen to all the other kids, parents, and teachers talk about what happened to my dad. My dad had to get another job. We had to move. I had to go to a different town, switch schools, switch football teams, get new friends—I was ticked. For a while I literally hated the people that made the decision to fire my dad and upend my life. I wanted something bad to happen to the principal and the boosters who were involved in that decision. The hurt was real. The anger was understandable. But giving in to the bitterness was wrong.

Fortunately, my parents had a series of conversations that helped me forgive the ones who hurt me. God actually used the experience to strengthen my heart and prepare me to fend off bitterness for the rest of my life. Even since becoming a pastor, people have done things that hurt my reputation. A few have questioned my integrity. Some have said things about me on the news or online. Occasionally people have said hurtful things about me to my wife or my kids. Of course, that stuff comes with the job—"If you can't stand the heat, get out of the kitchen." Nursing low-level bitterness and grudges is easy. Forgiveness is hard. But it's worth it. That's the lesson Christian parents need to teach our children.

The default posture of the sinful human heart is bitterness and brokenness. We have to teach our kids to choose forgiveness and restoration. They don't come naturally to us. Christian parents need to train our kids to defy the natural pattern and embrace the supernatural pattern offered by Jesus. One of the best ways we can do this is to model it. The cauldron of family life and marriage give us daily opportunities to model this behavior. Our marriages can be full of miscommunication, mistrust, misunderstandings, and mistakes. Forgiveness can be caught as much as it is taught. When our kids see a marriage or a mom or a dad who lives free from bitterness, they will see a model worth emulating. When children are raised in a repentance-rich home that is full of constant grace and forgiveness, they will be well prepared to extend the same to their outside relationships.

Parents Need to Model Repentance and Forgiveness toward Each Other

Jimmy and I (Kristin) are crazy about each other. We've been married for a long time and we are still grateful to get to spend our lives together. But we also do plenty of things that frustrate one another. Marriage is like that—it gives us ample opportunities to repent and forgive. When one sinner marries another sinner, they begin a cycle of constant repentance and forgiveness.

There is nothing more humbling than asking our spouse to forgive us. Sometimes we are afraid that if we ask for forgiveness, our spouse will think they are completely blameless. If we forgive them, they may forget how wrong they were and offend us again. That is a foolish way to think about repentance and forgiveness. We display such arrogance toward our spouse when we don't forgive. It's as if we are saying that *our* sins are far smaller and less significant than theirs.

Our kids will notice if we repent and forgive well. We want them to see us keeping short accounts and moving on. It will impact the way they treat their future spouses. Since our marriage is the first relationship our children see up close, we need to model a good and healthy one. We can only do that if we are good repenters and good forgivers.

Parents Need to Model Repentance and Forgiveness toward Our Children

I (Kristin) knelt down in front of my sweet little two-and-a-half-year-old boy, put his face in my hands, looked him straight into the eyes, and said, "Son, I am so sorry that I spoke to you that way. I was wrong. Will you forgive me?" I was a young mom in my early twenties, and had a lot to learn. That was the start of a long journey of being a repenting parent.

Repenting is an important aspect of parenting. We wish it were unnecessary. We wish we sailed through parenting our eight children. We would love to be able to wear the titles of "Perfect Mom" and "Perfect Dad." But that's just not the real world.

We cannot use our children's behavior as an excuse for our own. "I'm sorry I spoke that way, but you are getting on my nerves," is not an apology. When we repent, we own it. And that's it. Don't repent with an addendum. Just repent. It is humbling to ask for forgiveness, especially from someone who we are supposed to be teaching and training. But that's the point. We *are* teaching and training in those moments when we ask our child to forgive us. They will live lives full of opportunities to repent. We want to show them how to do it the right way.

- **We need to be the first and best repenters.** Our little kids will start out thinking that Mom and Dad are next to perfect. When we lash out at them, they will think that we are right and that they are the problem. If we don't ask for forgiveness when they are little, they will internalize guilt. We need to help them see the truth. On the other hand, when we blow up at our teenagers, they *know* we are wrong. They might not internalize guilt, but they might internalize anger. If we don't repent, our teenagers will notice, and they will be frustrated.

- **We need to be the first and best forgivers.** The same instance that made me (Kristin) a repenting parent also pointed out how I needed to be a forgiving one. My son was actually an example to me at that moment. When I asked him to forgive me, he did an amazing thing. He threw his arms around me, gave me the biggest and longest hug, and said, "I forgive you, Mommy. I love you SO MUCH." And that was it. No lecture, no hesitation, just sweet and simple forgiveness. I long to be that kind of forgiver. We want to parent in such a way that our children feel safe coming to us to confess when they have messed up. We want them to feel safe because they know we will readily forgive. They need to know that our love doesn't hinge on their behavior.

Actually, we should forgive our children before they ask. We will be sinned against as parents. We will be lied to, taken for granted, disrespected, and disobeyed. We must constantly remind ourselves that their sin is not a personal struggle between our children and us. It is not us versus them. Instead, it is a spiritual battle. We as parents do not want to respond in ways (anger, mocking, lecturing, unforgiveness) that make us a stumbling block to our kids. *Repent* and *forgive*. These are two important verbs for parents. We must lead the way.

Parents Need to Teach Our Kids to Repent Correctly

We have a rule in the Scroggins home. When you mess up, you can't just say, "Sorry." The one-word phrase, "Sorry," is not an acceptable way to ask for forgiveness; it's not really asking for forgiveness at all. It's just an obligatory word that we say to quickly move on from an uncomfortable situation. A true apology has three components: an acknowledgment of guilt, identification of the specific infraction, and a request to be forgiven. It would sound something like this:

> "Caleb, I'm sorry that I borrowed your basketball
> without asking. I left it at the park and now it's gone.
> I will get you a new one as soon as I make enough
> money. Will you please forgive me?"

OR

> "Mary-Claire, I am sorry for lying about you to
> Mom. I blamed you for something I did. I was trying
> to get out of trouble, and I threw you under the bus.
> Will you please forgive me?"

This is much more effective than, "Sorry"—wouldn't you agree? Repentance is more than saying words, but it is not less than that. Of course, we are concerned about the heart behind the words, but the words are still important.

We need to encourage our kids to say the right things in the right way. Do not allow them to shift their eyes around to avoid the awkwardness of the conversation. Teach them to look the one they have offended in the eyes as they deliver their apology. They will get plenty of practice asking for forgiveness at home if they have siblings. This training ground will help our kids learn to make things right with those outside of our homes, when parents aren't around.

Parents Need to Teach Our Kids to Forgive Correctly

Somehow, most of us tend to think that we have to wait to forgive until we feel like forgiving. We still feel hurt, angry, or scared, so we're not ready to forgive. But just like someone asking us to forgive them should not be a prerequisite to forgiveness, neither should our feelings. Obedience often requires us to do the right thing before we feel like it.

Holocaust survivor Corrie Ten Boom wrote about an encounter she had with a guard from Ravensbrück, the concentration camp where she and her sister were imprisoned. She had just finished speaking at a church when the guard approached her. He explained that he had become a Christian and that even though he knew God had forgiven him, he wanted her to forgive him on behalf of all the victims of his cruelty. She knew Jesus requires believers to forgive as we have been forgiven. She said, "And still I stood there with the coldness clutching my heart. But forgiveness is not an emotion—I knew that, too. Forgiveness is an act of the will, and the will can function regardless of the temperature of the heart." Ten Boom prayed for strength, thrust her hand into his outstretched hand, and cried, "I forgive you, brother." Then she wrote, "For a long moment, we grasped each other's hands, the former guard and the former prisoner. I had never known God's love so intensely as I did then."[3]

As Corrie learned that day, obedience almost always comes before feelings. Obey first. The feelings will follow. We do not forgive because we feel like forgiving. If we waited for feelings, we would seldom forgive. Like we said earlier, we need to teach our children that forgiveness is releasing the offender to the Lord. We forgive because the Lord has forgiven us.

> Obedience almost always comes before feelings.

As we point out God's design for forgiveness, Christian parents must teach our children to be thankful for the forgiveness we have received from God. We have to help them understand that the Lord does not give us the judgment we deserve. God lavishes love and mercy on us before we want it or even know we need it. The Bible says, "But God proves his own love for us in that while we were still sinners, Christ died for us" (Rom. 5:8). When our

---

[3] Corrie ten Boom, "Guideposts Classics: Corrie ten Boom on Forgiveness," *Guideposts*, posted on July 24, 2014, https://www.guideposts.org/better-living/positive-living/guideposts-classics-corrie-ten-boom-on-forgiveness.

children are grateful for the gospel, that attitude of thankfulness will help them to forgive others. A grateful heart is a forgiving heart.

Parents Need to Help Our Kids Deal with Bitterness Quickly and Decisively

This is not to say that we minimize things that happen to our children. They will experience real hurt, real betrayal, real disappointment, and real embarrassment. Listen to their stories and identify with them. Tell them that you are sorry for what they are walking through. You can let them know that you wish you could fix it and make things right. Sometimes the offense will be great enough that you do need to step in and defend your child. Most of the time, though, you have to love them, listen to them, and guide them through the process of forgiveness.

Parents must teach our kids the principle of keeping short accounts. Encourage them to go to the Lord immediately with their hurt. Pray with them for the one who has offended them. The Bible instructs us to do this. Jesus tells us this: "But I tell you, love your enemies and pray for those who persecute you" (Matt. 5:44). We would like it better if it said, "Talk bad about your enemies so that everyone around will know they stink." But it doesn't say that. Jesus tells us to love and pray for those who offend us the most because we are to show the watching world the character of our Father. We are his children who bear his image. We misrepresent him when we hold on to grievances. He loved us when we were unlovely. If we are going to be like him, we must do the same to other people. Holding on to grievances causes a root of bitterness to grow in our hearts. Jesus said, "You have heard that it was said to our ancestors, 'Do not murder,' and whoever murders will be subject to judgment. But I tell you, everyone who is angry with his brother or sister will be subject to judgment" (Matt. 5:21–22). We guess you could say Jesus takes unforgiveness pretty seriously.

A Sample Guide for Crucial Conversations

Relationships can get messy. If we interact with others, we will eventually have conflict. It's inevitable. Those conflicts, left unresolved, often lead to unforgiveness and bitterness. It is our task as parents to guide our children through the process of repentance, forgiveness, and restoration. We can only recover and pursue God's design for our lives when we understand and implement these concepts faithfully.

Daughter: "I'm so angry at her, Mom. She lied about me. She told the whole class that I cheated on the test, and I could tell they believed her. I can't stand her. I will never trust her again."

Mom: "I'm so sorry. I'm sure you were embarrassed. I'm not sure why she would do that to you. You've been friends for a long time."

Daughter: "Well, not anymore! I'm done with her."

Mom: "I get it. It hurts when people we care about embarrass us or betray us. Honestly, when I hear you talk about it, it makes me mad too. I don't like to see you hurting.

What are you going to do?"

Daughter: "I can forgive her and move on (not going to happen), I can ignore her, or I can talk about her and try to get everyone else mad at her. I don't know what to do. I'm so angry I can't think straight."

Mom: "I get it. I've been in that same spot many times. Sometimes when I am offended, I try to think how I would hope someone would treat me if I was the one in the wrong. I've been wrong plenty of times, and I am so grateful when people forgive me."

Daughter: "Yeah, me too. But why should I forgive her? She isn't even sorry."

Mom: "It would be nice if she would ask you to forgive her. But we don't get to pick how other people behave. We can only choose how we respond. I'm not saying you have to be her best friend, but I do think you need to forgive her. You are really only punishing yourself if you harbor bitterness toward her. Besides, God has forgiven you so much, right? That's the gospel. Jesus died for our sins before we asked for forgiveness. We have to forgive because we have been forgiven. Release her to the Lord. Do not take her punishment on as your responsibility. Be kind. Be wise when interacting with her. Right now, she probably isn't your best source of friendship. But you can always say hello and be kind."

These are tough conversations. They are especially difficult because parents do not like to see our children get hurt. Our instinct is to protect and defend. We hate it when the ones we love are wronged, and we want to seek retribution on their behalf. We tell our kids to forgive and be kind even as we struggle to do so. But we are compelled to forgive because of the teaching and example of Jesus.

CHAPTER 7

Friendship and Mean Kids

Awards become corroded, friends gather no dust.[1]
—Jesse Owens

I (Jimmy) felt the little squeeze on my index finger. The hand was tiny, but the grip was impressive. My newborn daughter had her fingers wrapped around mine, and she was well on her way to wrapping *me* around *her* little finger. Every time we brought a baby home from the hospital, I would look at their little faces and fingers and toes and think how gentle and innocent they appeared. Those children were completely dependent on Kristin and me to provide for their needs and to protect them from harm.

When children are small, the parents are their whole world. But it doesn't stay that way for long. Their circle of relationships will expand—first to siblings and extended family, then to

---

[1] Jesse Owens, GoodReads.com, https://www.goodreads.com/quotes/1018226-awards-become-corroded-friends-gather-no-dust.

neighbors and school friends; eventually, they develop an entire social sphere independent of Mom and Dad. That's life. We accept it. But we don't have to like it.

Our kids will make friends. Our kids will be influenced by their friends. Our kids will become like their friends. Because friendships are so vital, Christian parents must do everything we can to help our children cultivate healthy friendships. Good friends are a comfort in hard times. Good friends can encourage our kids to be heroic. Good friends make life more meaningful and more fun.

Perhaps the most famous Bible verse about friendship is what Jesus said about the sacrificial love that exists between true friends. He said, "No one has greater love than this: to lay down his life for his friends" (John 15:13). That is the kind of friendship God designed our kids to have!

Christian parents understand that training our kids to find the right friends is crucial. Training them to maintain and develop strong relationships with friends is part of the parenting task. The good news is our kids don't have to be the most popular people in the world—they only need a small circle of people that care about them. Some kids will struggle to connect with their peers. Other children will make friends naturally and effortlessly. Either way, parents must be intentional about training their children in the art of friend-making.

Training is necessary because friendships aren't easy—they are complicated. Along the way, our kids may have their hearts broken by people who didn't turn out to be good friends. Kids will be mean. Kids will be backstabbers. Kids will be rude. And kids will pressure other kids to do the wrong things. It's also not always the "other kids" that are the problem. Our kids may not always be perfect friends either.

Parents are going to have many conversations with kids about friendships. Some of these conversations will be challenging because parents will wonder if friend-struggles are normal growing-up stuff, or if the struggles are creating more serious emotional, psychological, or spiritual wounds. Parents are likely to encounter conversation starters like these:

- "I don't want to go to school because I don't have any friends."
- "Why don't you ever like my friends?"
- "When I hang out with those girls, they ignore me."
- "I tried to eat with them at lunch, but they didn't make room for me."
- "Every time I play with the neighbors, this one boy always comes over and picks on the rest of us. I just want to punch him in the face."
- "I don't know what to do when I'm hanging out with my friends and they start doing things I don't feel comfortable with."
- "I wasn't invited to the party."
- "Everybody at church is two-faced and fake."
- "I don't need any friends. You can't trust anybody anyway."

Like other issues addressed in this book, it would be impossible to anticipate every possible challenge with our kids and their friendships. But we don't need to—what parents really need is a grasp of God's design and a map for potential conversations. The Bible gives plenty of good instruction about managing relationships with peers.

God's Design for Friendship

One of the most famous friendships in the Bible is the friendship between Jonathan and David. Jonathan was the son of King Saul, and first in line for the throne—at least in terms of tradition and logic. David was the son of a farmer. But God had chosen David to be then next King of Israel. David was promised the throne by the prophet Samuel (1 Sam. 16:12–13). There was tremendous potential for rivalry between those two men.

Jonathan and David had several things in common. Both men were powerful warriors. Both men were famous for their exploits in battle. Both men were influential statesmen. Both men had a right to believe they would become the king of Israel. And both men loved God. When they were young, they lived in the royal household together—Jonathan because of his Dad's position, and David because he was invited into the palace after he killed Goliath and became a national hero.

For whatever reason, Jonathan and David just "clicked." When they met in the aftermath of the Goliath slaying, the Bible says, "Jonathan was bound to David in close friendship, and loved him as much as he loved himself" (1 Sam. 18:1). Pretty strong. But Jonathan and David weren't just friends out of convenience. When you read the Old Testament, you find out that these young men were actually committed to each other in a deep, life-giving, God-honoring friendship. Listen to some of the things they did for one another in the name of friendship:

- Jonathan gave David his personal, prized possessions. (1 Sam. 18:4).
- David and Jonathan promised friendship and loyalty to one another (1 Sam. 18:3).
- David married Jonathan's sister (1 Sam. 18:20–30).
- David gained spiritual encouragement from Jonathan (1 Sam. 23:16).
- Jonathan risked his life to protect David from harm (1 Sam. 20:24–34).
- Jonathan acknowledged that David would be king instead of him (1 Sam. 23:17).
- David adopted Jonathan's son after Jonathan died (2 Sam. 9).

Most of us will never know friendship like that. But Jonathan and David provide a powerful model for strong, loving, lifelong friendship.

Solomon had most likely heard of the friendship between his dad (David) and Jonathan. Perhaps that's what Solomon had in mind when he wrote about friendship in Proverbs and Ecclesiastes.

- **Friendship is necessary and valuable.** Ecclesiastes 4:9–12 says: "Two are better than one because they have a good reward for their efforts. For if either falls, his companion can lift him up; but pity the one who falls without another to lift him up. Also, if two lie down together, they can keep warm; but how can one person alone keep warm? And if someone overpowers one person, two can resist him. A cord of three strands is not easily broken."
- **Friends can make you better.** Proverbs 27:17: "Iron sharpens iron, and one person sharpens another."
- **We become like our friends.** Proverbs 13:20: "The one who walks with the wise will become wise, but a companion of fools will suffer harm."
- **Friends can become closer than family.** Proverbs 18:24: "One with many friends may be harmed, but there is a friend who stays closer than a brother."

Clearly, Solomon placed a high value on the quality of his friends. Since the book of Proverbs is addressed to his sons, we know that parental concern over friendships is supported by biblical precedent. We *should* be concerned over the people that our kids are involved with. We need to teach our kids to choose the right friends. We should also be intentional about training our

> We need to teach our kids to choose the right friends. We should also be intentional about training our children to *be* good friends.

children to *be* good friends. This means scads of conversations about how to cultivate and nurture healthy, supportive, and fun relationships. Our kids will develop friendship skills when they are young, but the ability to build dynamic friendships will bless them for a lifetime.

Sibling Relationships Are a Training Ground for Friendship

If you think about it, a lot of the relationships we read about in the Bible are sibling relationships. Unfortunately, there are a lot of negative sibling/friendship examples in the Bible:

- The first sibling relationship, Cain and Abel, ended when Cain's jealousy motivated him to kill his younger brother, Abel (Gen. 4:1–16).
- Jacob stole his brother Esau's blessing (Gen. 25:24–34).
- Joseph used his father's favoritism against his brothers (Gen. 37:1–11).
- Joseph's brothers retaliated by selling him into slavery (Gen. 37:12–36).
- Miriam and Aaron spoke out against their brother Moses's leadership (Num. 12:1).
- David's oldest brother, Eliab, berated him for wanting to challenge Goliath (1 Sam. 17:28).
- One of David's sons, Abasalom, killed his half-brother Amnon for raping his sister, Tamar (2 Sam. 13).
- And the list goes on.

You get the idea. It is unlikely that our children will take things to these extremes (thank goodness). But we have all seen sibling relationships wither and die due to rivalry, unforgiveness, and unrepentance. The Bible provides a lot of clear instruction about how believers in Jesus are to treat one another in our own families, in the family of God, and in all of our human relationships/friendships. God tells us to:

- Love one another (John 13:34; Rom. 12:10).
- Honor one another (Rom. 12:10).
- Live in harmony with one another (Rom. 12:16).
- Build up one another (Rom. 14:19; 1 Thess. 5:11).
- Care for each other (1 Cor. 12:25).
- Serve one another (Gal. 5:13).
- Carry one another's burdens (Gal. 6:2).
- Forgive one another (Eph. 4:1–2, 32; Col. 3:13).
- Be patient with one another (Eph. 4:2; Col. 3:13).
- Be kind and compassionate to one another (Eph. 4:32).
- Comfort one another (1 Thess. 4:18).
- Encourage one another (1 Thess. 5:11).
- Consider one another in order to provoke to love and good works (Heb. 10:24).
- Pray for one another (James 5:16).

The best place to start training kids in the art of friendship is in the home. When we cultivate strong sibling relationships in our own home, we are setting our kids up for success in all future friendships. Siblings are the only friends we have for life. Brothers and sisters have a unique set of shared experiences. They are the only ones that really know where we came from and how we grew up. They don't *need* a backstory. They *are* the backstory.

Family relationships are the first building blocks of our identity. Even before we are able to acknowledge our connection with God, we understand mother, father, sister, and brother. Family bonds can enhance or detract from the way we view God and how we fit into his plan. Our brothers and sisters help shape who we are and what we think about ourselves and those around us.

Our job as parents is to create an environment where our kids don't see themselves as competitors for attention, affection, and resources. Instead, we want them to see their siblings as friends who share responsibility for each other, for the family name, and, ultimately, the cause of Christ. Parents can't make siblings cultivate strong relationships with each other. We can't force them to be best friends. We can't require our adult children to stay connected. We *can* foster a healthy environment for sibling relationships to flourish. We *can* communicate to our children how important and valuable their siblings are. We *can* create an atmosphere that facilitates strong ties of love, commitment, and interdependence among family members.

You may be thinking that it's easy for us to talk this way since we are married with eight kids. But we want to assure you that it's possible for anyone in any family configuration to strive for God's design. If you think your family is messed up, just read the Bible stories referenced above! Every family is messy. Every relationship is messy. The more complicated or unique your family situation is, the more intentional and creative you will need to be. You can find the right people to be "permanent friends"—that is, friends who are unlikely to fade out of your life because of petty quarrels or normal, everyday interpersonal friction. You can find a core group of "safe people" that will love your child for who they are, accept them unconditionally, and give them freedom to develop the skills and the art of friendship. You can work to create networks of like-minded families to help you. Perhaps those relationships exist in your extended family or in your church family. Depending on your situation, finding and keeping these kinds of relationships may be difficult. But you can still do it.

Developing an environment where sibling relationships thrive requires intentional conversations between parents and our kids. How can we, as parents, manage our children toward this kind of friendship?

Work Hard to Build a "Team" Mentality

When our first five boys were younger, our backyard was a wreck. Toys were often scattered to and fro. The trampoline net sagged because they always leaned on it. The grass wouldn't grow because there were always five sets of feet running and jumping in the same patches day after day. Our yard received a lot of wear and tear. I (Kristin) didn't care. I didn't mind because I loved watching my tribe bond over games of football, kickball, Wiffle Ball, dodgeball, and a bunch of other games they made up. The yard was a beautiful mess to me. I loved everything our tired and struggling backyard playground represented. The brothers spent hours together in that yard playing and getting into mischief. They were competitors, but they became a team.

Over time, "Team Scroggins" developed a reputation in the church, in the school, and in the community. Everyone who knows us knows "Team Scroggins" rolls deep. There are a lot of us, and we take care of each other. Our children are all close and enjoy being together. We are so thankful for that. They *choose* to be best friends now. Do they still argue? Yes. Do they get annoyed with each other? Of course. But they are a team. They keep up with each other. They cheer for one another. They defend and protect one another when necessary. They rejoice together in the good times and pick each other up when times are hard. A friend recently asked our youngest son what he was most proud of about our family. He said his favorite thing is how we are super loyal to each other. I love that!

This idea of "team" is valuable when proactively building healthy sibling relationships. Team members don't have to be good at the same things, think the same way, or have the same likes and dislikes. Team members are united because they are part of the same unit and represent the same group. They have a deep sense of responsibility for each other and are moving toward the same goal together. Talk a lot with your children about being a team. We say it over and over again—"Team Scroggins!" You do the same with your family name. Over time, "Team" will start to sink in.

Train Your Kids to Think of Others

When you have eight children, you have to teach them to share from the very beginning. You really have no choice. We don't live in a mansion—we live in a normal-sized home. None of our children have their own room. They pile in on top of each other. That's normal life for them. We have discovered that tight spaces can actually be a blessing. Tight spaces force kids to share toys, rooms, and resources. Now that some of them are older, they share vehicles. They have to share time with Mom and Dad and each other (one-on-one time with parents and siblings is rare, and highly valued). But we are trying to teach them something more important than just sharing spaces and resources. We are trying to teach them to think of others.

"Thinking of others" is the goal. "Sharing" is one of the tools we use to train children to think of others. The Bible says Christians should put others before self. The apostle Paul wrote, "Do nothing out of selfish ambition or conceit, but in humility consider others as more important than yourselves. Everyone should look not to his own interests, but rather to the interests of others" (Phil. 2:3–4).

When our kids were small, we figured out that we needed to develop some family rules. We had seen other parents with rules posted on their refrigerators, bulletin boards, etc., and parents used these rules to train their children. Some of these folks had *a lot* of rules. Some of these rules were *very* specific. For example, "Don't use your sister's markers without asking." We had so many children that creating rules about kid-specific minutiae didn't make much sense. We came up with just *a few* rules that would be easy to articulate and remember, but would cover a "multitude of sins." Our house rules are: (1) Respect authority, (2) Tell the truth, and (3) Think of others.

Notice that this idea about thinking of others is so important that we made it one of only three family rules. It is a biblical principle that has real-life applications. If we had a nickel for every time we have said, "think of others" to our children, we would be millionaires. Most sinful behavior involves selfishness. Our fifth grader left clothes all over the floor? Think of others. Our high school junior didn't bring the car home in time for our college freshman to go out on a date? Think of others. Took your dad's phone charger without asking? Think of others. We actually cannot think of one sin that doesn't have self-centeredness at its root.

You might be saying, "You think those are *sins*? Take it easy!" We do think those actions are sinful, because selfishness is always sinful and contrary to God's design. Of course, you scale the intensity of follow-up conversations to match the degree of selfishness and the impact on others. But kids need to be reminded of the brokenness that results from selfishness. They need to be trained on how to repent and be restored, even in the "little things." Kids should be encouraged to forgive small things easily and restore generously. Teaching these things to children requires *thousands* of conversations. That's why "think of others" is such a vital principle for Christian parents to teach their kids, especially if you want them to build healthy friendships.

When our first son went off to college, he attended West Point. He called home one night and said, "You know how you drilled into us the idea of thinking of others? Well, we make fun of it and get tired of hearing it sometimes, but don't quit saying it. It's important. I understand the importance of it now more than ever. Because I know how to think of others, my transition from home to Academy life has gone a lot smoother."

Our children aren't always going to be under our roofs (we hope) or sharing rooms with siblings. They will eventually have teammates, roommates, coworkers, and spouses. Thinking of others will make those relationships richer and help our kids grow up to be the kind of friends that God wants them to be.

Teach Your Kids to Cover Over Weaknesses

When you live in the same house, you are very familiar with one another's weaknesses. You know the weird things they do, the bad habits they have, and the things about which they are particularly sensitive. If the sibling dynamic is bad, brothers and sisters highlight one another's weakness and cover one another's strengths. But in healthy friendships, you do the opposite. Love demands that we highlight strengths and cover weaknesses.

> Love demands that we highlight strengths and cover weaknesses.

Love "does not keep a record of wrongs" (1 Cor. 13:5). We think that covering over one another's weaknesses is a gospel principle. The Bible says Jesus *understands* our weaknesses (Heb. 4:15–16), died to *cover* our sins (Rom. 4:7), and *cancels* the record of our sin-debt to God (Col. 2:14–15, emphasis added).

In teaching this principle, we are not asking our children to cover up problems or to pretend they don't exist. We are simply encouraging them to highlight the strengths of their siblings and not to dwell on their struggles. If there is something they can do for their sibling to fill in the gaps for them, they should do it. For example, one of our sons knew his little sister struggled with being away from home. She was in the third grade and still felt a little nervous about being away from Mom and Dad. When it was time to go to Kid's Camp with our church one summer, big brother (a fifth-grader) asked our Children's Pastor to put him and his sister on the same team. The big brother didn't make fun of his sister in front of their friends for being nervous. He just came alongside her and was there for her. Now that's being a good friend!

Tattling on one another is the opposite of covering over weaknesses. If you have more than one child in a room, there will probably be tattling. If those two children are brothers or sisters, there will *definitely* be tattling. "Mom, she won't share." Or, "Dad, he's looking at me." We even had one of our sons run down the stairs to announce, "Mom, the brothers are calling me a tattle-tale." Tattling is annoying. That's enough of a reason to put a stop to it. But the real reason to curtail tattling goes deeper than that. Tattling isn't just wearisome to the ears. Tattling indicates something wrong in the heart. Selfishness is the root of most tattling.

I (Kristin) happen to have some of the smartest friends. My good friend Apryl has three daughters. When her girls tattled on each other, she asked them this question: "Are you telling me this to get your sister *in* trouble or to get her *out of* trouble?" Brilliant! Those are two very different motives. One answer indicates an attempt by the tattletale to manipulate the situation to get her own way. The other answer stems from a true concern for the other person.[2]

The same goes for unnecessary teasing—especially when outside the home. All siblings have "inside stories" on each other. A lot of those stories are based on legitimate struggles that one of the siblings may have. The sibling with the struggle may not mind a little teasing about it in the privacy of home, but would be discouraged and embarrassed if the siblings mentioned it to people outside of the family. This is another area where the team mentality kicks in. Team builds up. Team protects. Team takes on the problems and concerns of the other members. Families need to "circle the wagons" and have one another's backs. Teach siblings to love the other siblings for the best things about them. Some may not naturally get along, but they can still love each other, cheer each other on, and cover each other's weaknesses. When they learn to do that, they will have the building blocks for true friendship.

---

[2] My friend originally got this from Berenstain Bears.

Facilitate Intentional Time Together

I (Kristin) was in the kitchen preparing lunch one day. I looked up and saw two of our boys—six and seven years old—walking up the stairs with their arms around one another. They were headed up to play in the room they shared. My heart melted. Did they get in a fight a few minutes later and come back down to tattle? Yes. Remember complexity? Still, I loved seeing them being kind to each other in that moment. It was genuine and real. Just two brothers—the best of friends—choosing to spend time with each other.

Our girls have shared a room since the youngest was one year old—basically, their whole lives. They argue occasionally. They borrow each other's stuff. They each blame the other if the room gets too messy. But that constant proximity has created a pretty intense bond. They help each other "get ready" before they go out. They share similar tastes in movies and music. Sometimes it is difficult for us to get them to quiet down and go to sleep. We often hear them through the walls giggling together in the night. This ordinary (and necessary) process of learning to share a room is building memories and a friendship that will last a lifetime. It is also teaching them how to be a good friend to future roommates, housemates, and spouses.

It would seem like spending time together with siblings who live in the same house would be unavoidable. How could you grow up in a house together and *not* spend time with each other? Well, it's surprisingly easy. Being in the same space does

---

not always equal spending *quality* time together. Creating *quality time* for siblings requires intentionality and is increasingly countercultural.

Our American society is structured to help our children—and our families—live separate lives. Siblings often have their own spaces, devices, and preferences. They are in different grades. They may attend separate schools. When they go to church, they might be divided into age- and gender-specific groups. They will have different interests and abilities and inclinations. Facilitating time together will take work on your part, but the return on your investment will prove profitable.

> Being in the same space does not always equal spending *quality* time together.

When all eight of our children were under the same roof, we implemented "sibling time." It was a designated time of the day or week for the kids to spend time with one of their brothers or sisters. We actually had a rotation so that as the weeks went by, they spent an equal number of "time-slots" with each one of their siblings. We also set it up so that older kids would have to take some responsibility for the younger kids. During sibling time the older sibling would give the younger one three choices and the "little sibling" got to choose which one they would do. They could play a game together, work on an art project together, or learn a new skill together. No electronics were allowed. It had to be an activity that caused them to talk to and make eye contact with each other.

One of the benefits of sibling time is the special connection that has developed between kids of widely varying ages. For example, our youngest especially loved sibling time with his oldest brother. The older one hasn't lived in our house for over five years. He's married and is a dad himself. But the younger one still calls his big brother his "best buddy." They are thirteen years apart.

Although it looks a little different these days, sibling time is still a thing for our family. Now it looks more like FaceTime calls, group chats, and planned family vacations. As parents, we don't have to structure it or facilitate it as much anymore. The kids do it because they want to. They do it because they are actually friends. The family is a great training ground for lasting friendships.

The concept of "sibling time" may not resonate with you. Or perhaps you don't think it will work in your context. That's fine—it's just an idea. We bet you can come up with your own strategy to build friendships between the children in your home. It's likely that some of your kids will naturally feel close to each other. It is also completely normal if some have challenges making a strong connection. The goal is that our children do not see each other as annoyances or interruptions; we want them to learn to see each other as friends.

Create Shared Experiences

When we were young parents, a mentor told us: "When it comes to your children, don't invest in giving them *things*. Invest in giving them *experiences.*" When we were in college another mentor told us: "You will never grow as a person except for the places you go, the people you meet, and the books you read." We have benefited greatly from that advice, and now we pass it on to you. One of the best ways to build friendships in any arena is to go places together, meet people together, and read books together. That's what we have tried to do in our family. You could try it in yours.

Some of our favorite family memories involve family trips. We have made two cross-country treks together. We've seen the Grand Canyon, the deserts and mountains of California, the Pacific Ocean, and the Hoover Dam. We've traveled to Washington, D.C., Philadelphia, and New York City. The experiences we had on those trips were invaluable.

Shared experiences don't have to include traveling to far-off places. Reading books together as a family isn't expensive or terribly time consuming. We have read all kinds of books together, from The Chronicles of Narnia to The Great Brain series to The Little House on the Prairie books. Reading those books gives our kids a shared storehouse of characters, sayings, and plotlines.

An easy-to-create shared experience is having someone over for a meal so that your children get to know them and learn from them. We have had neighbors, people from different backgrounds, coaches, teachers, seminary professors, and missionaries in our home. We coach our kids up before dinner so they will ask good questions like:

- "What do you do for a living?"
- "How did you decide that is what you wanted to do?"
- "How did the two of you meet?"
- "What's the favorite place you have ever lived? Why?"
- "If I want to grow up and do what you do, how would I get started?"
- "How did you become a Christian?"

Having them prepare questions and role-play (especially when kids are younger) ahead of time has helped our children be ready to make good conversation with our guests. Some of the crazy conversations our kids have in those settings are permanent parts of our family lore.

Most of the shared experiences your kids will have with each other are rather mundane, but they are experiencing even the ordinary things *together*. Shared experiences are special because shared experiences create shared memories. Memories last far longer than things. Things break, wear out, and go out of style. Not memories—they become richer and more meaningful over time.

Make Faith Part of What Bonds Your Kids Together

Any parent should want to train their kids to build healthy friendships. And any parent would agree that strong sibling relationships are desirable and powerful. But *Christian* parents have an added advantage and an additional obligation when it comes to sibling relationships and friendships. We have an *advantage* because the gospel actually creates a spiritual bond and connection that transcends the bonds of earthly family or friendship.

If our kids are believers, their *spiritual* brotherhood and sisterhood goes deeper than connections forged by shared DNA or earthly adoption. Plus, the Holy Spirit will help our believing children live out the fruit of the Spirit (Gal. 5:22–23) as they learn to love and live with one another. As Christians, love for one another is not optional—it is a command of Jesus (John 13:34–35).

Christian parents who are trying to raise Christian kids should put our faith and the gospel at the center of our parenting, sibling relationships, and training for healthy friendships. Obviously, having gospel-centered, 3 Circles-type conversations can help. But there are lots of other ways we can integrate our faith into the fabric of our family relationships. We can:

- Read the Bible together and have family devotions.
- Faithfully attend church together as a family.
- Serve the poor, the sick, or the less fortunate together.
- Save up and go on a mission trip together.
- Pray for our neighbors together.
- Discuss sermons or Bible lessons together.
- Discuss books, movies, or television shows together. (What do they communicate about faith and life's big questions?)

These are just some of the ways we've tried to involve our Christian faith in our closest relationships. Shared experiences will help bond your kids together. Shared *faith experiences* will help put roots to their faith while deepening their love for one another. We have found that a shared faith, shared spiritual experiences, and a shared commitment to pursuing God's design can help build friendships between our children, even if they are very different from one another.

We encourage you to work at it. Teach your kids to be close. Remind them to cheer for each other and help each other. Praise them profusely when you see them "friending" with one another. If your kids learn to be good friends with their siblings, they can learn to form healthy friendships outside the home for the rest of their lives.

Talking to Kids about Friendships

Almost all of the concepts we teach our children about sibling relationships will apply to friendships at large. Using our homes as a training ground will set our children up to have lasting and meaningful relationships with others outside our walls. When dealing with sibling relationships, parents have a lot of control and input. Once the kids walk out the front door, the training in this "controlled environment" will be tested. Beginning with extended family members and preschool, our kids will have friends move in and out of their lives throughout their growing-up years. As a parent, you will have innumerable conversations about friendships. You will warn your kids about dangers, suspicions, and heartaches that arise from friendship challenges. But those conversations will likely be balanced by experiences of love, support, and loyalty from excellent friendships your kids cultivate.

In our experience, some of the most difficult parenting conversations center around three issues: choosing the right friends, navigating difficult friendships, and dealing with mean kids. Fortunately, God has a design for all of it!

Help Your Child Choose the Right Kind of Friends

When your children are little, choosing the right friends is easy. The truth is, when you are dealing with preschoolers— parents really choose friends for their kids. You connect with people that *you* enjoy spending time with, and if those people have children, then your kids automatically have friends. But as your children get older, their peer groups aren't necessarily tied to you. They have teammates, classmates, neighbors, and other relationships that you may not even be aware of. So how do you help your children choose the right kinds of friends?

Honestly, the work you do in helping them *be* the right kind of friend will transfer over to them *choosing* the right kind of friends. As you teach your children the importance of honoring God, thinking of others, and covering over weaknesses, they will begin to see those qualities (or the lack thereof) in others. Because they have been trained to have the right kind of friendship values, your children will tend to be attracted to the right type of friends.

But sometimes they won't choose the right kinds of friends. Kids feel a great need to belong. They want someone to sit with at the lunch table. They don't want to be the loner who has a hard time finding their "group." As parents, we want our kids to fit in too. Sometimes our kids may be tempted to join the wrong type of people just so they can feel like they fit in *somewhere.* Therein lies the danger. Remember what Solomon wrote to his sons? "The one who walks with the wise will become wise" (Prov. 13:20). So far, so good. If our kids will make friends with wise people they will become more like their wise friends. Solomon had more to say though: *"But* a companion of fools will suffer

> Our kids are likely to become more and more like the people they hang around. This is why choosing the right friends is vital.

harm" (Prov. 13:20a). Solomon knew what we as parents know— our kids are likely to become more and more like the people they hang around. This is why choosing the right friends is vital.

One time when I (Jimmy) was in high school, there was a big fistfight between two kids during the school day. It was quickly broken up, so they didn't get to finish duking it out. As the two teenage pugilists walked away, they both vowed to meet later that afternoon and finish what they started. Word spread, and by the time school was out, it seemed like the entire student body headed out to the prearranged spot. I knew these were rough kids and the fight was happening in a rough neighborhood. And I knew I should stay away. But I didn't. I was hanging out with a bunch of other boys who wanted to go, and so we all went.

When we arrived, one of the kids ended up pulling out a gun and threatening his opponent, then waving it around randomly at the crowd of onlookers. You have never seen a bunch of high school kids dive for the ground and run for their cars so fast. The police got involved. There were arrests. Fortunately, nobody got hurt. And nothing of consequence really happened. But that was a dangerous situation I could have easily avoided. But I didn't, because I was with the wrong crowd in the wrong place doing the wrong thing. "A companion of fools will suffer harm" (Prov. 13:20b).

That kind of situation is exactly what Solomon is talking about. This is why when our teenage kids bring friends to the house, we try to connect with them. We want to look them in the eye and hear a little bit about their stories. Most of the time our kids choose wise friends. We are usually impressed and think, *If you hang around him, he will help make you wiser. Good choice!* But every once in a while, our kids bring home a knucklehead. We can see them coming a mile away. That's when we think: *Watch out—if you hang around her you will suffer harm. That is one of the fools Solomon was warning you about.* We don't always say everything we are thinking. Parents have to use discretion about what to say and when to say it. Preferably, we wait until our kids bring something up to us. Guiding our kids through the minefield of wise and foolish friends requires consistency and persistence on our parts.

When having conversations about friend choices, be sure to talk with your children about the importance of having their closest friends be ones who will help them do what is right. Proverbs 27:17 says: "Iron sharpens iron, and one person sharpens another." Our children need friends who will build them up and encourage them in their faith. But these kinds of friends don't grow on trees. They have to be sought out. These relationships need to be cultivated. Your church family is a great place to look for like-minded families and solid, godly, young people. Friendship opportunities are one of the reasons we place a high value on strong children's and student ministries in our church. Kids need a "fishing pond" for friendships.

Even if you are talking with your kids and even if you have a strong connection with your church, there may be seasons where your kids seem like they are in a "friend drought." Sometimes it will seem like there are no positive influences for your kids to connect with. That's okay. Keep talking. Keep looking. And keep asking God for help. Pray with your child and ask the Lord to bring this type of friend to them. At the right time, God will do it.

Help Your Child Navigate Difficult Friendships

In a perfect world, all of our children's friendships would be edifying and uplifting. But none of us live in a perfect world. Although our children's *closest* friends should be their siblings and others who build them up, every relationship they have won't fall into those two categories.

Our children will sometimes have friends and acquaintances who have different values than theirs. They may be friends with people who are not like them at all and who may even try to get them to do things that are contrary to their faith and ideals. Sometimes it's not a clash of values, but rather a lack of chemistry. Some kids just don't click. It's not anybody's fault. You can't force friendship.

Every kid will have relationships where they are *required* to interact and function politely and productively. They will need to manage these "mandatory friends" whether or not they have similar values or good chemistry. What kinds of relationships are we talking about?

- Teammates, classmates, and other extra-curricular co-participants
- Kids of their parents' friends
- Kids at church
- Neighbors that you see frequently
- Extended family members (cousins, etc.)

How can we coach our kids to make the best of "mandatory" relationships that they do not enjoy? And even if they do enjoy the acquaintance, how can we help our children to create environments that are most conducive to avoiding compromising their values and fostering positive interactions?

- **Coach your kids to avoid being judgmental.** Try to find the balance between maintaining your values and not getting "preachy" with the other person. Since you are the parent, make sure you do not speak negatively about these other children. If you do, your son or daughter may either resent your attitude or see your negativity as permission to express their own.

- **Coach your kids to find neutral ground.** "Neutral ground" means finding places to hang out that will not put your kid at a disadvantage. You want them to be able to express themselves or have input into activities, topics of conversation, or starting and ending times for the meetup. Think meals, malls, parks, etc. By "neutral ground" we also are referring to "relational catalysts" like music, books, games, sports, movies, etc. As much as you can, insist on choices that would be acceptable or enjoyable for everyone involved.

- **Coach your kids to bring activities to "your turf."** Your home, your church, or your neighborhood. When arranging playdates, get-togethers, or special events, seek to be the host instead of the guest. When you or your kid is seen as the host, you have significantly more control over what is talked about, what activities are available, and how people are treated.

- **Coach your kids to enjoy the best things about these acquaintances, and to try to avoid focusing on shortcomings or points of friction.** Just because your child doesn't see eye to eye with another kid doesn't mean there aren't good things about that person to learn from or enjoy. Remember that the other kid is complex (just like your kids). Time in these situations is mandatory, but limited. If we can train our children to see the best in others, they will have better attitudes, better experiences, and better relationships.

These types of mandatory friends and acquaintances are unavoidable—literally everybody has them. Your children will need your help if these relationships get tricky. But these relationships can be valuable. Invest in them and encourage them. Draw the other kids close if you can. Your family may be able to influence them for Christ.

> When arranging playdates, get-togethers, or special events, seek to be the host instead of the guest.

Help Your Child Deal with Mean Kids

Mean kids have always been around. They make movies about them. There are memes and GIFs portraying them. If you have lived any amount of time, you have met at least one. Some of us have been the mean kid.

As Christian parents, we want to teach our kids to be kind to those who aren't kind to them (Luke 6:35). Our kids should do everything they can to coexist peacefully with others (Rom. 12:18). As Christians, our kids should even be willing to endure *more* from mean kids than most people would expect (Matt. 5:38–42). Of course, we want to recognize that mean kids are complex too. They are mean for a reason. As believers in Jesus, we should care about *them*, even if they are mean to us. The

Bible says we should pray for our enemies, love our enemies, and do good to our enemies (Matt. 5:44). But the Bible also acknowledges reality. Paul said, *"If possible, as far as it depends on you,* live at peace with everyone" (Rom. 12:18, emphasis added). Sometimes your kids will do everything they can to live at peace. But the mean kids won't have it.

After praying, loving, turning the other cheek, and going the extra mile, some of those mean kids just keep on being mean. If your kid is the target of a mean kid, you may feel helpless. You will almost certainly feel angry. You will want to step in and protect. It may come to that, but we recommend you try some other avenues first. You will definitely need to have parenting conversations with your child about attitude, words, and strategy. Because what you *can't do* is expect your child to simply endure endless bullying, harassment, and humiliation.

The best thing to do to mean kids is ignore them. Get away from them if possible. The problem with mean kids is they often will refuse to go away. They are in constant pursuit of victims. You can teach your kids to tell parents or the teachers or the coaches what is going on. But mean kids tend to be experts in evading accountability. The one who tells will likely be labeled a "tattle-tale" and may become even more of a target. Parents have to teach our kids a strategy for dealing with persistently mean kids.

One of our sons was at the basketball courts in our neighborhood one day when he was a little boy. While playing there with a group of other children, he encountered a mean kid. This kid was a young teenager, nearly six years older than our son. He pushed our son down. He called him names. He cursed at him. He stole his bike. All in front of the other neighborhood kids, which was humiliating. This kid knew there was nothing our guy could do. The boy was bigger, older, and stronger than our son. Now, the kid had the bike and wouldn't give it back. He kept riding the bike in circles around our crying son and continued to make fun. The mean kid thought he had gotten the best of our boy. He had—at least for the moment. What this kid didn't know is that our son had brothers.

Our little boy cried angry tears all the way of the one-and-a-half-mile walk home. As soon as he came through the front door, we all knew something was wrong. His brothers made him tell them what had happened. They were mad. At our house, no one messes with the siblings and gets away with it.

The two oldest brothers had their little brother walk the neighborhood with them looking for the kid. They found him. When the brothers confronted the boy, he wouldn't give the bike back. He refused to apologize, made excuses, mocked little brother some more, and then told the big boys he was just joking around and that it wasn't a big deal. "It's a big deal to us," they said. "You don't pick on our little brother. You're a bully. You're not going to treat our family like that." And then they wore him out. They gave him a good old-fashioned whooping. Not to the degree of serious injury, but just enough to make their point. They got the bike back and their little brother rode home with a huge smile on his face. That smile had nothing to do with the bike and everything to do with the fact that his brothers had his back.

Some of you may not agree with us on this, but we encourage you to let siblings defend each other from the mean kid. Teach your children to stand up *to* the bullies, and stand up *for* the vulnerable. Our kids should not seek to get in fights (we don't want our girls to fight at all, ever!). If your child can use words and warnings to diffuse the situation, that's the best. Every conflict does not need to result in a fight. We want our kids to try to resolve conflicts with as little force as necessary. Sometimes, however, they are going to have to take the bully down.

Here is the formula we teach our younger boys (up through middle school) when it comes to dealing with bullies:

- Always try to use your words first.
- Tell the bully to stop whatever it is they are doing.
- If they don't stop, say: "If you don't stop, I will make you stop."
- If they still don't stop, do whatever it takes to stop them. Push them, punch them, kick them, tackle them. Do your best.
- Only use the minimum amount of force necessary to make your point.
- If you choose to fight the bully—know he may win the fight.
- We think it is usually better to resist than to be bullied. Bullies pick on the weak and they don't like to pay

a price. If you push back hard enough, they are likely to move on.[3]

Of course, kids need to learn wisdom when confronting bullies. There are times when the best course of action is for our kids to remove themselves from the situation. There are other times when the bully is truly dangerous, and parents and other authorities need to get involved. The older our kids get, the bigger and stronger the bullies get, and the more dangerous the confrontations can become. That is why for high school kids and older, I do not recommend fighting at all if it can possibly be avoided. Still, sometimes boys (and men) are called upon to fight. Parents should help their boys be prepared for challenging situations, to discern the wisest course, and then to take action. Make sure your kids know that standing up to bullies is not only acceptable, it is right and honorable.

> Standing up to bullies is not only acceptable, it is right and honorable.

The *ultimate goal* would be to win over the mean kid and help him change his or her mean heart. Jesus can do that. Jesus does

---

[3] If you're thinking, *Wow, this seems over-the-top or unkind*, we understand that not everyone may agree with us here. With that said, the steps are pretty similar to the long Christian tradition of Just War Theory, broken down and applied to a family and sibling context. They are never to instigate a fight, only to respond in self-defense or defense of a more vulnerable person. They should exhaust all peaceable solutions. They should announce their intentions. And they should use the minimum amount of force necessary.

it all the time. Matthew, Zacchaeus, and Paul were all grown-up versions of "mean kids" before they met Christ. But they were all changed by the gospel. We want to make sure that the way our kids and our families respond to mean kids and bullies leaves the door open for repentance, forgiveness, and restoration. The greatest result of these conversations and interactions would be for the mean kid to one day become a friend.

A Sample Guide for Crucial Conversations

Son: "I don't get along with him, Mom. We have nothing in common. He's such a pest. When my friends come over today, I want him to leave us alone."

Mom: "I agree that the two of you are very different. You like different things and you have different personalities. I do think you have more in common than you think."

Son: "I just don't get why he wants to hang out with me so much. He needs to make other friends."

Mom: "I understand your frustration, but let's be fair. He has plenty of other friends. You, however, are his best friend because you are his brother. That's the way it should be. He looks up to you and wants to be with you. Don't push him away because you two are different or because you get irritated with him. Pull him in for a little while when your friends are over today. Include him and be kind. Treat him like a best friend and not like an annoying little brother.

I will get him involved in another activity at some point while they are over so that you can have some time with your friends."

Son: "That won't help because he will get mad when I tell him to go away. He won't listen."

Mom: "Well, no one likes to be told to 'go away.' What is a better way you can handle that?"

Son: "I don't know. I guess I can just include him in what we are doing. If I let him join us, maybe he won't be so annoying. I think he tries to bother us because he feels left out. It's not like my friends hate him or anything. They would be fine if he hung out with us while we play outside. He's actually pretty good at basketball."

Mom: "I think that's a great idea. Your friends are choosing to come to your house. They know you have a little brother. If they really didn't want to be around your brother, they wouldn't come over. But if they were to treat your brother wrong, you shouldn't put up with that. Brothers come first. Don't treat your friends better than you would treat your brother. You can be a good friend and a good brother at the same time."

My (Kristin) dad was one of the most loyal men I have ever known. He worked for the same company for his entire career. He was a decorated Marine and a Vietnam vet. He loved my sister and me unwaveringly and was so proud of his ten grandchildren.

He absolutely loved Jimmy and treated him like a son. He was married to my mom for almost fifty years before he went to heaven.

My dad was the oldest of three sons, and he loved his brothers. I grew up hearing about how he tried his best to care for them. He had some crazy stories! He, being the oldest, felt a great sense of responsibility to take care of his brothers. He would defend them at all costs. My dad learned to be a friend to others by cultivating friendships with his siblings.

When my dad died after a long and grueling battle with cancer, we were struck by the number of people who came to his memorial service. Several of them we didn't even know. They were people my dad had worked with, ministered to, led to the Lord, bailed out of hard situations, sat with while their family member was dying. As each one paid their respects, they would say to our family: "Your dad was so good to me. He was a loyal friend and I am grateful to have known him." Person after person filed by with similar stories. Dad spent a lifetime building relationships with his brothers and his friends. He took care of those who were struggling. He defended those that needed an advocate. He was an example of a true friend.

I want to be that kind of friend. We pray that our children will learn to be friends like that. If they will *be* the right kind of friends, they are more likely to *attract* and *cultivate* the right kinds of friendships. It takes conversations and practice to help our children develop the skills to have the right types of relationships. Parents need to be up to the task.

Mom and Dad, the conversations you have with your kids about God's design for friendships will prove valuable to your children as they are growing and learning. We want the siblings in our home to move toward genuine and loyal friendship. And we want our children to develop other friendships that are healthy and strong. Don't get discouraged if your children don't seem to buy into these concepts after a single conversation. Remember to think "management." Siblings will love being together one minute and be annoyed with each other moments later. Our children will be the best of friends with someone one day and be angry with them the next (especially if you have girls). The idea of management will help you press forward as you train your children and work through friendship issues.

CHAPTER 8

A Guide for Any Crucial Conversation

*Let your speech always be gracious, seasoned with salt, so
that you may know how you should answer each person.*
—Colossians 4:6

*A word spoken at the right time is like
gold apples in silver settings.*
—Proverbs 25:11

Our goal for this book was to share a pattern for having gospel-
centered conversations with your kids about any topic. Each
chapter includes some information and some sample conversations,
but there is no possible way to be truly comprehensive. We
wouldn't even know *how* to address every potential situation you
will face with your children. We *do* know that parents are dealing
with a lot because *we* are dealing with a lot. One of our kids has
been diagnosed with obsessive-compulsive disorder, and we have

had to navigate that. Some of our kids have learning disabilities, and we have to figure that out. A couple of our kids experience mild depression and pretty serious anxiety from time to time. We have been foster parents of children who truly lived through trauma; their trauma became our responsibility. Some of you may have kids who have suffered some form of abuse. There are a myriad of issues and challenges that come up over the course of a child's life.

As parents, we need a plan—a road map for these vital interactions with our kids. This is why having a biblical framework and conversation *guide* is so crucial. You can process any crucial conversation through the lens of the 3 Circles. Even if you don't draw it out every time, and even if you don't explicitly *mention* the 3 Circles concept, having the diagram in your mind can help you avoid getting stuck or sidetracked. This road map will keep the conversation moving toward restoration and ensure that you include crucial elements to get you there.

Of course, most real-life parenting conversations will not contain the entire 3 Circles paradigm. It's okay if you need to work through one aspect of the conversation in one sitting and then pick it back up later when the time is right. The key is that you, as a parent, are not grasping at straws or flailing around looking for something to say. No matter what the issue is, no

> No matter what the issue is, no matter how surprised you may be, and no matter how awkward the timing—you have a plan for any conversation that needs to be had.

matter how surprised you may be, and no matter how awkward the timing—you have a plan for any conversation that needs to be had.

Here are a few things to keep in mind as you have these crucial conversations with your children.

Praise Your Child(ren) for Confiding in You

Your child is taking a risk every time he or she brings hard-to-handle topics to you. No matter how difficult or troubling the question may be, it's a good thing that our children are asking these questions, and an even better thing that they are asking *us*. We want to work hard to keep the lines of communication open. We need to let them know that we are willing to talk to them about *anything* and that they can always come to us.

> God's design is the remedy for any brokenness.

As our kids get older, their questions get more challenging. We need to be careful about how we respond. Parents need to develop a good poker face. Sometimes our kids may ask us questions that are alarming, sad, or embarrassing. We can't concentrate on that part of it. Instead, remember that God's design is the remedy for any brokenness. Focus your mind on his good design and his redemptive plan. Parenting is not for wimps, and God has made you tough enough for these conversations. No matter what, our kids need to know that we are *glad* they have come to us for help.

Ask Questions for Clarity If Necessary

We like to be quick with our answers. We're the parents, after all. We're the ones who are supposed to have it all figured out. The Bible, however, cautions against this way of thinking. The Bible says, "Everyone should be quick to listen, slow to speak, and slow to anger" (James 1:19). Of course, we know Jesus was a master at answering a question with a question. (There is a great example of this in Mark 10:17–18.) When your child brings an issue to you or when you have to raise an issue with your child, it is always wise to ask questions. Let them do some talking. This is where you can get insight into what is going on in their hearts. The goal is to get at the heart of the issue. It also gives you time to think about how you are going to respond. Sometimes getting our kids to talk to us is like pulling teeth. Don't get frustrated if they don't talk to you. It's okay. God will bring to light everything you need to know at the right time.

Affirm Their Feelings and Point to God's Design

If your child does reveal to you how they are feeling, take the opportunity to affirm them. You can say, "So I hear you saying that you were really hurt when your friend didn't invite you to the mall," or, "I understand how angry it makes you when your brother cheats." Once you have expressed affirmation, you may want to turn the conversation toward God's design.

We always want to start and end with God's design when addressing problems, issues, and concerns with our kids. God's design is clearly articulated in his Word. You may have noticed that we started each chapter by outlining the biblical principles that applied to each topic. We know that it might not seem fair since we are in ministry and have been doing this for a long time. But we want to encourage you that you are just as capable of learning what God says about any given topic as we are. If you are a believer, you have the Holy Spirit filling you and guiding you. He is your teacher (John 14:26) and your guide (John 16:13). You have your church family to help you understand the Scriptures and give you practical advice. (If you don't have a church family—find one ASAP!)

There is no more important job or ministry than training our children's hearts. It is worth the time and effort to study the Bible and discover God's design for every area of our lives. This is also where your church family comes in. When you don't know what to do or where to turn, we encourage you to lean into your pastors and to connect with other parents whose kids are in a similar stage of life. We like to say that our church family is The Home Depot for parenting—"You can do it. We can help!"

Tie Their Feelings of Concern to the Idea of Sin and Brokenness

Let's face it—most crucial parenting conversations happen because our kids are experiencing brokenness. They have done something wrong or have been wronged. They are sad, mad, or have been "bad." They are hurt and they need our help to find healing. They are probably experiencing shame and guilt to some degree. Every measure of brokenness that we experience is ultimately the result of sin—either our own sin or the sins of others against us (sometimes it's a combo). We want to help our kids see the relationship between brokenness and sin.

Move from Brokenness to the Gospel

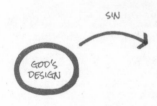

The goal of crucial parenting conversations is to teach our kids the gospel by constantly reminding them of the gospel. The gospel is simply this:

- Jesus came to this earth as a man and lived a perfect life. The Bible says that he was tempted just like we are, but he never sinned—not one single time (Heb. 4:15).
- Jesus died on the cross for our sins. The sins of the world were laid on him as he hung on the cross (1 Pet. 2:24; 1 John 2:2) because the penalty of sin is death (Rom. 6:23).

- Jesus was buried (Matt. 27:57–61).
- Jesus rose from the dead paying our sin debt (Col. 2:14–15) and defeating death on our behalf (1 Cor. 15:54–55).
- Every person is invited to repent of their sins and believe the story of Jesus (Mark 1:15).

This is the gospel. Of course, there is more that could be said about the gospel and as you have hundreds of conversations with your children you will bring in different aspects of the gospel story. Every problem, issue, or concern that we have can be addressed by the power of the gospel. The gospel is the power of God to save and bring healing to every possible situation.

> The gospel is the power of God to save and bring healing to every possible situation.

As parents we can't anticipate every variation of conversation that will arise with our children, but we can prepare for the fact that these conversations are coming. Reminding ourselves of the gospel will help us keep things in perspective and not lose heart when our children struggle. It is important not to lose heart because they *will* struggle. The gospel gives Christian parents confidence that brokenness is not the end of the story.

Move Toward Restoration

We have to continually remind our kids that God never gives up on them. If they are believers in Jesus, then the Holy Spirit lives in them and he is at work making them more and more like Jesus (Rom. 8:29). Our goal as parents is to continually show our kids the way to recover and pursue God's design for their lives. It means turning from the sin and consequences of the sin, receiving the forgiveness that is theirs in Christ, and asking the Holy Spirit to help them live according to God's design. It means choosing God's way over our own way and then doing it again and again.

We talked about the importance of restoration in chapter 6. Depending on how deep the brokenness is, restoration may look different. If you know that your child has become involved in deeply rooted habitual sin, part of the restoration process may call for an accountability process and/or a biblical counselor. Your church family may need to get involved. Your church may have people who specialize in helping parents and children work through challenging issues. If not, perhaps a pastor or church leader can refer you to a competent Christian therapist. The point is that we can't always just pronounce restoration—we have to help our children work toward recovering and pursuing God's design.

The 3 Circles originated as a gospel-sharing tool, but the principles apply to the whole of our Christian lives. As long as we live on this flawed earth with flawed people in our flawed families, we are going to find ourselves in places of brokenness. When we or our children fall down, we have to remember that Jesus *always* wants to pick us up. No matter how deep the brokenness goes, it is *never* too late to recover and pursue God's design.

Don't Forget "Complexity" and "Management"

Keep in mind the ideas of complexity and management that we talked about in the first two chapters. These ideas will help you as you navigate conversations with your children. Our children are complex and so are we. Even when we see them struggling, we must remember God's goodness in them and remind them of the ways God is working in their lives. Some situations can't be solved with a "one and done" conversation or decision. Some temptations don't go away just because we had a "3 Circles" conversation. There are challenges in life that have to be managed. Remembering the concepts of complexity and management will help our kids press forward. It will help us press forward too.

Intentionality

Being intentional with our parenting is key. We actually feel like we could have written this book in two sentences: "Be intentional. The End." But the question really is: "How?" How can we be intentional?

Conversations are a great place to start. Whether you are having "proactive" or "preventative" conversations initiated by you, or "reactive," "triage," "brokenness" conversations initiated by them, the 3 Circles give us a map to navigate these conversations. You aren't going to work your way through all 3 Circles every time. That would be overwhelming for you and your child. If you try that, they may quit talking to you! It is still a great way to order your conversations with them. The ideas of God's Design, Sin and Brokenness, and Repentance and Restoration will guide you as you engage with your children on a multiplicity of important issues.

Play Long Ball

Parenting is a lifelong endeavor. We have to play long ball. No one experience, episode, or conversation is going to be the answer. But over time, God will use us to shape the ways our children view him, the world around them, and their place in it. Take heart, parents! Just as you are *for* your children, our God is for *you.* And God is especially for you as you fulfill your responsibility to train and disciple your kids.

My (Jimmy) dad is a godly man and an exemplary father, father-in-law, and grandfather. He always says that the test of your parenting isn't how your children turn out—it's how your *grandchildren* turn out. Are you able to parent in such a way that *your* children are successful in passing God's truths on to *their* children?

We are writing this book, but our parenting hasn't really been tested. Although at the time of this writing we have two married children, we are far from empty nesters. We still have two college students, two high-schoolers, a seventh grader, and an eleven-year-old. We still have hundreds and hundreds of conversations yet to have with our "in house" kids. And that doesn't even count the conversations we are having with our adult children.

As we were wrapping up the final chapter of this book, our first grandchild was born. It's a boy. We flew out to meet the new addition to our family face-to-face. Of course, we were so proud of our oldest son and daughter-in-law, and we wept tears of joy when we held their son in our arms. It was kind of amazing and surreal to watch *our* boy take care of *his* boy. Seeing him take care of his little family makes *us* feel like we have accomplished something good. We have another grandbaby due in a few weeks. Our second son and his wife are having a girl. We are absolutely thrilled. And now, according to my dad, the true test of our parenting begins.

> This is the true test of Christian parenting—will the next generation know God? Will the *next generation* tell *their children*?

The psalmist wrote: "He commanded our ancestors to teach to their children so that a future generation—children yet to be born—might know. They were to rise and tell their children so that they might put their confidence in God" (Ps. 78:5–7). This is the true test of Christian parenting—will the next generation know God? Will the *next generation* tell *their children*? Will multiple generations of our descendants set their hope in God?

That's the point of parenting conversations. That's the point of the 3 Circles conversations. That's the point of this book. Our desire for ourselves, and our children, and our grandchildren is that we all will set our hope in God. Our desire for *you*, and *your* children, and *your* grandchildren is that *they* would set their hope in God.

Parenting isn't easy. But God will help you. Your church family will come alongside you. The task is difficult. But it's possible.

Parenting is not for wimps. You can do it!

MORE
3 CIRCLES
RESOURCES

Turning Everyday Conversations into Gospel Conversations

Three Circles
Teen Study Bible Book

also available

The Plan, the Fall, and the Very Good News: A Bible Story Collection
Kids ages 6-10

Available where books are sold